The Future of America's Political Parties

The Future of America's Political Parties

Edited by Andrew E. Busch

LEXINGTON BOOKS

A division of
ROWMAN & LITTLEFIELD PUBLISHERS, INC.
Lanham • Boulder • New York • Toronto • Plymouth, UK

LEXINGTON BOOKS

A division of Rowman & Littlefield Publishers, Inc.
A wholly owned subsidiary of The Rowman & Littlefield Publishing Group, Inc.
4501 Forbes Boulevard, Suite 200
Lanham, MD 20706

Estover Road
Plymouth PL6 7PY
United Kingdom

British Library Cataloguing in Publication Information Available

Library of Congress Cataloging-in-Publication Data

The future of America's political parties / edited by
Andrew E. Busch.
   p. cm.
 ISBN-13: 978-0-7391-2072-9 (cloth : alk. paper)
 ISBN-10: 0-7391-2072-7 (cloth : alk. paper)
 ISBN-13: 978-0-7391-2073-6 (pbk. : alk. paper)
 ISBN-10: 0-7391-2073-5 (pbk. : alk. paper)
 1. Political parties—United States. 2. Politics, Practical—United States. I. Busch,
Andrew.
 JK2265.F88 2007
 324.27301'12—dc22   2007028969

Printed in the United States of America

♾™ The paper used in this publication meets the minimum requirements of American
National Standard for Information Sciences—Permanence of Paper for Printed Library
Materials, ANSI/NISO Z39.48–1992.

Table of Contents

Acknowledgments   vii

Preface   ix

Introduction   *Charles Kesler*   xi

1.   The Democrats' Strategy for the Future   1
Elaine Kamarck
Roundtable Discussion: Peter Beinart, Patrick Caddell,
Elaine Kamarck, Nelson Polsby, and Ruy Teixeira

2.   A New Direction for the Parties?   35
Honorable Timothy Roemer

3.   The Republicans' Strategy for the Future   49
Andrew E. Busch
Roundtable Discussion: Michael Barone, Andrew E.
Busch, Hugh Hewitt, and William Kristol

4.   The Parties and Campaign Finance   83
Michael Malbin

5.   The Future of Party Organization   99
Nelson W. Polsby

6.   Cultural Issues and the Future of the American   107
Party System
William G. Mayer

Index   121

About the Participants   125

Acknowledgments

First and foremost, I would like to thank the Salvatori Center for the Study of Individual Freedom in the Modern World. The Salvatori Center sponsored, funded, and staffed the Conference on the Future of America's Political Parties which serves as the basis of this book. Specifically, I would like to acknowledge Charles Kesler, Director of the Salvatori Center; Elvia Huerta, whose organizational contribution was invaluable; and Kris Anderson, who led a team of Claremont McKenna College students who performed much of the tedious work involved in setting up the event. Jack Pitney performed yeoman service as the moderator of the Democratic panel, as did Charles Kesler as moderator of the Republican panel. I would also like to thank Kay Mead, our intrepid transcriber, for her efforts. My dear wife Melinda spent hours formatting the manuscript for publication, with help from Christine Oldham and Tracy Fontan at Claremont McKenna College. Joseph Parry and Lynda Phung of Lexington Books were both helpful and patient. And, of course, there would have been no conference without the contributions of our superb line-up of participants.

Preface

On April 7, 2006, the Salvatori Center for the Study of Individual Freedom in the Modern World at Claremont McKenna College hosted a conference on the Future of America's Political Parties. It was a moment of great uncertainty for the parties. In the wake of the 2004 presidential and congressional elections, Democrats struggled to find a winning message, one that would excite their liberal core while offering an image of strength abroad and cultural moderation at home. For their part, many Republicans were dispirited, sensing that their party had lost its way and was no longer exercising power on behalf of principled purpose.

Democrats looked to the November 2006 midterm elections, then exactly seven months away, with cautious anticipation, Republicans with creeping dread. When the votes were counted, the elections clarified some matters—the Republicans had indeed been in serious trouble—but left many other questions that would continue challenging the parties over the following two years, in some cases more severely than before. Democrats won a referendum against the Bush administration, but had refrained from offering a coherent alternative vision. Republicans could be sure that they needed to engage in reflection about the future of their party, but the elections did not provide certain answers about what that reflective process should yield. In most respects, the challenges of April 2006 were still the challenges of April 2007, for each party. In addition, a variety of questions touching both parties were not going to go away any time soon. How would the parties finance themselves under the still relatively new rules of the 2002 Bipartisan Campaign Reform Act (BCRA)? How would the parties structure themselves organizationally to compete in the future? How would they approach the minefield of the cultural issues?

The conference brought together a number of respected and dynamic political analysts—some of them fine scholars, others noted and thoughtful commentators—to address these questions. This book is a compendium of the papers and the discussions flowing from that effort.

After introductory remarks by the Salvatori Center's Charles Kesler establishing a framework for the day's discussion, a panel on the future strategy of the Democrats included a paper by Professor Elaine Kamarck and a discussion featuring Kamarck, *New Republic* editor Peter Beinart, long-time Democratic consultant Patrick Caddell, Professor Nelson Polsby, and analyst Ruy Teixeira. On the same lines, a lunchtime address was delivered by former Congressman Timothy Roemer (D–Ind.), who had briefly sought the chairmanship of the Democratic National Committee after the 2004 elections.

A complementary panel on the Republican strategy for the future began with my paper on the subject, followed by a roundtable that added the inestimable Michael Barone, radio commentator and author Hugh Hewitt, and *Weekly Standard* editor William Kristol.

In addition, three noted scholars presented papers on broad topics of interest to the parties. Professor Michael Malbin, executive director of the Campaign Finance Institute in Washington, D.C., offered his assessment of how the parties were adapting to BCRA and presented an early glimpse into the potential for Democrats to do quite well in the House elections. Professor Polsby returned to deliver a presentation on the future of party organization. When Professor Polsby passed away in February 2007, it was clear that this conference was one of the last he had participated in through his illustrious career. Last but not least, Professor William Mayer analyzed the relationship of the parties, and of liberal and conservative activists, to the divisive cultural issues.

As you will see, the conference provoked spirited discussion, thoughtful insights, and a thorough overview of the key challenges facing the parties. For students, scholars, and citizens seeking to understand the state of the parties not just on the cusp of the Congress-changing 2006 elections but for the foreseeable future, this is a good place to start.

Andrew E. Busch
Editor
April 2007

Introduction

Charles Kesler

Among the prime constituents of freedom in the modern world are the political party and the system of party competition that is now almost a synonym for democracy. No one would consider a country democratic today that allowed no political parties, or that allowed only one. Two is fine. More than two is European, which is, of course, suspicious.

But political parties were not always even this respectable. George Washington counseled our young republic to beware the spirit of party, which tended to magnify minor differences, he said, to clog the administration of government, to sacrifice the common good to a partial good, and to threaten our union. And he knew what he was talking about, having presided over the onset of the first and probably the most bitter and divisive party battle in American history. This was the famous contest between the Federalists and the Democratic Republicans that culminated in the election of 1800.

But America developed a genius for turning partisan divisions into new grounds of unity. Political parties have divided us in order to reunite us in 1800, in the elections around the Civil War, and after the Civil War, the great election of 1932, which ushered in the New Deal coalition. The question that this conference addresses is whether the parties are still capable of functioning in this manner, the constitutional manner that George Washington might even have approved of. Contemporary political parties can certainly divide us, of that there's no doubt. But are they capable of generating a new consensus, a governing majority for the next generation or more? If so, which political party can do it, and how would it surmount the differences and deep divisions over such issues as the war, immigration, entitlements, sexual morality, and even the meaning of America, itself? We'll see.

Chapter One

The Democrats' Strategy for the Future

Elaine Kamarck

*Roundtable: Elaine Kamarck, Peter Beinart, Patrick Caddell,
Nelson Polsby, Ruy Teixeira*

The problem with advising or even predicting a political strategy for the future is that we are, inevitably, stuck in the past. The temptation to make a linear prediction from the most recent presidential elections is always powerful and often wrong. And yet the past is the only thing we know for sure and so, in an exercise like this one, we can't help but start there and grope forward.

The creation of a successful political strategy is based first, on a core set of values that distinguish one political party from the other—although in the American system the distance between these values is often not very great. It is also based, of course, on a set of facts, frequently disputed, about the party's immediate past and a set of assumptions, also frequently disputed, about the nation's future and what it means for politics and government. And finally, assumptions about whether the base of a political party is constant or changing and how, are critical to the crafting of a successful strategy since any successful party strategy has to proceed with the acquiescence, if not the enthusiastic support, of its base.

In October, 2005, my long time colleague Bill Galston of the Brookings Institution and I published a long analysis of the Democratic Party's immediate past and what it meant for its future.[1] This paper starts where that analysis ends although without the valuable assistance of Professor Galston. Hence, all its problems are my own.

Applying this crude methodology—core values, past experience and future assumptions about the country and the base of the Party—leads me to lay out, for purposes of discussion, five simple components of a successful strategy for the Democratic Party.

It is currently fashionable to bemoan the state of the Republican Party which has, since the 2004 election, been on a dramatic and largely self-inflicted slide into unpopularity. But it is currently also fashionable to bemoan the state of the Democrats and to note that they don't seem to be benefiting from the trials and tribulations of the Bush Administration. None of this will be sorted out until the votes are counted in 2006 and in 2008 but it is useful to note that the picture for the Democrats is neither totally bleak nor totally bright. Of the five strategic points to be elaborated below, numbers one and two reflect real strength and consensus within the party; the remaining three reflect areas where the Democrats have much work to do. Thus a five point strategy as follows:

1. Go simultaneously left and right on domestic policy.
2. Give "competence" another try; this time it may work.
3. Get a coherent foreign policy that protects America.
4. Stop trying to justify bad behavior with good policy.
5. Get right with God.

Go simultaneously left and right on domestic policy.

In spite of recent electoral failures, the Democratic Party as a whole still retains a substantial reservoir of trust among the electorate when it comes to domestic and economic policy.[2] These roots are deep, they go all the way back to the enormous amount of government innovation that took place under President Roosevelt and later under President Johnson when the Democratic Party created the modern social safety net. Social Security and Medicare are its crown jewels but Medicaid, unemployment compensation and the Earned Income Tax Credit are but a few examples of the way in which the Democratic Party has fought to redistribute wealth and provide security for average people within the context of a vibrant market economy.

By the 1990s, members of the Clinton Administration and many other Democrats were realizing that the social safety net was frayed; it was built for a different time and in need of adaptation to the realities of the emerging information economy. In the days before the Monica Lewinsky scandal consumed the political capital of Clinton's second term there was much talk, formal and informal, within the administration of modernizing the social safety net— including social security. With the stock market sky high, attention turned to various options for introducing some sort of private savings into social security. Serious policy reviews were conducted within the White House, and Vice President Gore personally reviewed the options to see if he wanted to discuss some new way of providing social security in his coming presidential campaign. Meanwhile in the Senate, Joe Lieberman, one of the most conservative Democrats in the Senate, reviewed privatization plans as well.

The Democratic flirtation with social security privatization ended with moderate and conservative Democrats concluding that it simply could not work. Even the modest "2 percent" privatization plan (a version of which the Bush Administration briefly dangled before the public) would either subject the elderly to a higher degree of risk—thus undermining the entire notion of social security—or end up with the government taking on so many guarantees that it would create greater costs for a system that was already having solvency problems.

In retrospect, the flirtation of the Democrats with social security privatization helped clarify one of the Party's core values. When President Bush made partial privatization the centerpiece of his second term domestic agenda the entire spectrum of the Democratic Party could and did unite in opposition. In less than one year the proposal was dead. Not bad for the Party that couldn't shoot straight.

Looking forward it seems safe to make two assumptions about the American economy that will allow Democrats to build on their strength in this area. First, it is clear that private sector pensions are going the way of the Model T. Recently it seems that you can't open the newspaper without some large corporation; IBM, Alcoa, Northwest Airlines, US Airways, to name a few, either freezing its traditional pension plan or declaring bankruptcy in time to get out of their obligations. Newer companies don't even bother to offer defined benefit pension plans. Against this backdrop a guaranteed old age insurance benefit and some sort of government assistance to those left out of the 401k world will be critical.

Second, the domestic context for health care is changing rapidly. Not only does the middle class fear, with great justification, that the next job might come without health care—but, even more important is the fact that the business world (correctly or not) is beginning to view employee sponsored pensions and health care programs as a competitive disadvantage in a global economy. Last December Ford Motor Chairman Bill Ford told the media that his company can compete with Toyota "but not with Canada" meaning that the government funded health care and pension policies of the Canadian government had made the U.S. less competitive as a manufacturing center.[3] When Toyota announced its decision to locate new production facilities in Canada in March the decision was widely understood as a comment on the high cost of employer health care in the United States. And the Canadian Industry Minister David Emerson bragged that Canadian workers were, on average, $4.00 to $5.00 cheaper than their U.S. counterparts, in part because of the lower costs of taxpayer funded health care.[4] Another frequently quoted factoid says it all—GM and Ford complain that the first $1500 of the price of every new automobile goes to pay the health care expenses of its retirees.[5]

Increasingly corporate America, long an opponent of the federal spending that would come with national health care—wants out. Assuming that these trends are more than passing the time is coming when Democrats can offer national health insurance as part of a pro-business platform! The Kerry presidential campaign laid out one important component of such a plan—the assumption of catastrophic care costs by the federal government. Other elements, such as a mandate that everyone would have to purchase health insurance, have been around for a while, thanks to the British scholar Stuart Butler.[6] The Federal Government could give everyone a tax deduction (or credit) for the purchase of health insurance, remove the tax advantages in the current employer based system and mandate that everyone purchase a health insurance plan. A similar system will need to augment the old age savings of low income workers without 401K plans. A rough version was outlined as part of Al Gore's 2000 presidential campaign.

By this time the reader will be wondering what the admonition to go simultaneously left and right means, given that I have just advised sticking with the current Social Security system and a form of national health insurance. These and other issues having to do with the creation of a robust social safety net should be coupled with a radical pro-growth policy—one that seeks to promote and reward investment, innovation and productivity. For many years Democratic support for strong social programs was coupled with hostility and suspicion towards big business. Much of this was fueled by the labor movement. But the labor movement has failed so far to adapt itself to the information economy. In spite of the efforts of some creative and forward looking leaders a very small number of American workers are now part of the labor movement.[7] In the future it is not unrealistic to predict that labor union members will occupy a smaller and smaller portion of the American workforce; as they do they will constitute a less important portion of the Democratic Party's base. This will free up the Democratic Party to make sensible pro-business decisions such as removing special interest tax breaks from certain sectors of the economy in favor of across the board corporate tax breaks. It will also free up the Democrats to propose fundamental left wing reforms in the social safety net in the context of a pro-business global competitiveness strategy. Hence the Democrats have a unique chance to go both left and right on domestic policy.

Give "competence" another try.

In the 1988 presidential election, Michael Dukakis was pilloried—rightly—for running a soulless campaign whose message consisted of the phrase "It's not about ideology, it's about competence." But times change. That was before the Federal Government's response to Hurricane Katrina so overwhelmed us with its incompetence that America was humiliated before the world. The response to Katrina, however, was only the most dramatic in a long series of implementation failures, from the planning of the war in Iraq, to the failure of the occupation, to the design of the Medicare prescription drug policy. At the Kennedy School of Government where I teach, we have traditionally begun the required course in government management with a case study on the Chicago heat wave of 1995 where hundreds of people died before the government even knew what was happening. The message we try to convey to our students of government was brought home to the entire country in September of 2005—when the private sector fails to manage organizations well, people lose money; when the public sector fails to manage well people die.

Hurricane Katrina was one of those "teaching moments" unlike any we've seen 9-11 and before that since the government shutdown in early 1996. The American reflexive hostility towards the very existence of government was, for a moment at least, put aside, as people understood that sometimes you actually needed the government to work. No one thought that the private sector could have rescued New Orleans.

For decades now, Democrats have suffered under the political albatross of being the party of big government. But in 2001 a Republican President inherited a budget surplus; by 2008 a Republican President and a Republican Congress will have bequeathed record budget deficits. Numerous conservative think tanks and scholars have pointed this out as well as Democrats.[8] So just who is the party of big government these days? And, perhaps more importantly aren't we entitled to some competence for all that money?

Just as Democrats had no trouble agreeing on a message of opposition to social security privatization, they've had no trouble agreeing on a message about the incompetence of the current government. Focusing on competence allows those Democrats who voted for the war and those who voted against the war to have a unified message. No wonder that the opening of the Democratic response to the 2006 State of the Union focused on competence. The new Governor of Virginia, Tim Kaine, summed up the argument as follows: "You know, no matter what political philosophy you hold or what state you call home, you have a right to expect that your government can deliver results."[9]

Republicans will try to argue that the Bush deficits are all about military and homeland defense but the Cato Institute, not exactly a bastion of liberal apologists, has shown the fallacy of that argument. Looking at spending policy back to President Johnson, Stephen Slivinski says "Contrast that with Bush's presidency so far. He has presided over massive increases in almost every category. This is a dramatic change from previous presidents, when increases in defense spending were offset by cuts in non-defense spending."[10]

Going forward, Democrats should morph their image as the party of government into the party of government that works. They should put together a robust reform agenda that focuses on the adaptations the federal government needs to make to protect America in this new era starting with a simple but powerful proposal—take FEMA (the Federal Emergency Management Agency) out of DHS (the Department of Homeland Security.) A government reform agenda can do for the Democratic candidate of 2008 what "reinventing government" did for Bill Clinton in 1992, show that he or she is attuned to the fact that government needs to work better and more efficiently than it does now. This was an important message for Clinton to deliver in 1992 since it helped him show people that he was a "different kind of Democrat." In 2008 a new version of that message, reworked around the theme of government competence, will be a welcome change from the record of the previous Administration.

Get a coherent foreign policy that protects America.

The flip side of the Democrats' reservoir of trust on domestic policy is a deficit of trust on foreign policy, in particular on questions of which party is best able to protect America.[11] In recent American history the Democratic Party has rarely been seen as the party of strength. Substantial parts of the base of the Party were shaped by protests against the war in Vietnam and never recovered. Many Democrats remain reflexively against American military action. This image of the Democrats as weak on defense is so pervasive that in the 2000 election Al Gore's proposed five year budget included $100 billion more dollars in military spending than did George Bush's proposed budget—and no one noticed.

The Clinton years provided no real opportunities to change this image. With the exception of the conflict in the Balkans there were no major military interventions and compared to Iraq, intervention in the Balkans imposed minor costs in both manpower and dollars. For most of the Clinton years, the Democratic deficit on security simply didn't matter. And then 9-11 gave a Republican President the opportunity to define the first chapter of the new "war on terror."

The 2002 midterm elections and the 2004 presidential election were wake up calls to the Democratic Party. In a post 9-11 world there is no hiding behind domestic policy. In 2002 Democrats made two critical mistakes. First, they thought that they could put Iraq and national security behind them by encouraging Democrats to vote for the Iraq resolution in order to run on a platform of prescription drug coverage. In our recent paper on the Democratic Party, Bill Galston and I refer to this as "the myth of prescription drugs."[12] Second, they allowed the Republicans to nationalize the election when they failed to realize that holding up passage of a Department of Homeland Security over protection of union rights for civil servants was a big loser compared to national security.

In 2004 both John Kerry and his running mate voted in favor of the war and then against the funding—a pair of votes guaranteed to sow confusion and contempt for the ticket. Kerry's consistently convoluted explanations of his war vote and his subsequent funding vote provided grist for the mill for the Republican Party.[13] To the critical swing voters it conveyed a Party that had no real plan for securing America—a catastrophic problem in the post 9-11 world.

There are some Democrats who wish that the security issue would just go away. But the ongoing war in Iraq and the tensions unleashed by it practically guarantee that the United States will be in a defensive posture in parts of the world for years to come regardless of the outcome in Iraq. There is simply no way of getting around the fact that Democrats need a coherent narrative about America's place in the world and the appropriate use of American power. Simply critiquing the Republican narrative and pointing out the misjudgments on Iraq will not do. The strategy needs to come to grips with the reality of American global hegemony and the need to defend America. It also needs to encompass a more modern view of national security; one that includes environmental and health degradation right up there with terrorism, conventional armed threats and nuclear threats. And it needs to support substantial expenditures on intelligence and military assets.

None of this will be an easy sell within that portion of the base of the Party that objects automatically to American military interventions. But there is a political precedent for what needs to be done. In 1991 and 1992 Bill Clinton discussed and argued his case in favor of welfare reform to a different part of the Party's base—African Americans. His frankness bought him acquiescence in the base. And to those looking at him from outside the Party, his discussion of welfare reform illustrated an admirable courage and independence.

Presidential candidates in 2008 will be well advised to talk about American military strength and to discuss America's inevitable obligations in the world in the primaries as well as in the general election. To a certain extent they can tailor this discussion to the base. There are those who, while they abhor military conflict in general, might applaud an intervention in the Sudan, for instance, where a bloody and brutal war has created a staggering humanitarian disaster. It is clear that there are military options to disasters like the ones that occurred in

Rwanda and in the Sudan but that these have rarely been planned for, trained for, or budgeted for.[14] But fundamentally, the Democrats must be seen as willing and able to use American military force in the world in protection of American interests and in an aggressive war on terror. They cannot fool themselves into thinking that the present widespread opposition to the Iraq War means that they can retreat into a pacifist crouch when it comes to engaging the world. The fact that many Democrats believe the Bush Administration has made the world less safe instead of more safe does not excuse them from the need to be able to exercise strength in the world.

Finally, there is a great deal of consensus within the Democratic Party on the need for a more robust Homeland Security. As the meteoric crash of the Dubai ports deal illustrated, the country does feel vulnerable. However, Democrats will be tempted to substitute homeland security for discussion of foreign policy and military affairs. It should be resisted. The vulnerabilities in American's homeland defense should constitute a portion of the competence argument in favor of the Democrats; they should not substitute for a strong foreign policy.

Stop trying to justify bad behavior with good policy.

In picking candidates Democrats will have to come to terms with the fact that in modern presidential politics the messenger is the message. Presidential elections are intensely personal. Time and again, broad descriptions of a candidate's personal qualities—strength, honesty, trustworthiness, matter more to voters than "the issues." The blogosphere has intensified the tendency to cover candidates like we cover movie stars; it allows for everything from insightful reporting to malicious gossip. In politics the message is the messenger. Democrats need to pay attention to the personal qualities of their candidates. Most people understand bad behavior more easily than they understand bad policy. Democrats have to find themselves messengers that do not interfere with the message.

It is extremely difficult to pinpoint exactly why Al Gore lost the 2000 election—especially because he won the popular vote. However, there is evidence that the Clinton scandals undermined support for his Vice President among liberal and moderate voters. In 2000 liberal and moderate voters who thought that the moral climate of the country was on the wrong track were 25 percent more likely to vote for Bush over Gore and liberal and moderate voters who thought that the scandals were very important were 40 percent more likely to vote for Bush over Gore.[15] In addition Gore did 6 percentage points worse among married women—the so-called "soccer Moms" of 1996—than Clinton had done.[16]

The movement away from the Democrats among married women accelerated in 2004 and was attributed to the greater desire for security among women. A phenomenon dubbed "the security Moms." But research by Anna Greenberg and Jennifer Berktold, presented in the table below indicates that "moral values" ranked even higher than security among the reasons why married women voted as they did.

While partisans of Bill Clinton argue fiercely that his behavior does not matter, it simply defies common sense to suggest that his sexual misconduct had no lasting effect on the Democratic Party especially when the memories of this scandal are kept alive in the popular culture as a constant source of jokes on late night television. The other most widely revered figure in the Democratic Party is Senator Ted Kennedy. And yet he, like Clinton, has been, in the past, morally challenged. Countless Republican campaign consultants have been able to conflate bad behavior into bad policy and to run against a Democratic Party whose leaders don't seem to live by the same rules as the rest of us. In fact, they seem to live by Hollywood rules, which might be fine for movie stars and rock stars, just not for politicians.

This problem is both easier and harder to solve than some of the other problems mentioned in this paper. Clearly Democrats need to find flag bearers whose personal morality will not overwhelm their message. More than one Democratic activist told former Senator Gary Hart that he should not pursue the Democratic nomination in 2004. Since he aborted his 1988 presidential run as the result of a sex scandal, Hart has been a prescient messenger on issues such as terrorism and homeland security. But no one wanted to let Republicans use the adultery card—again.

Table 1.1. Most Important Issue in Determining Presidential Vote (percent responding)

Issue	Unmarried Women	Married Women
The Situation in Iraq	25	21
The economy and jobs	18	15
Terrorism and National Security	13	18
Moral Values	13	27
Social Security and Medicare	7	4
Affordable health care	6	4
Education	6	3
The federal deficit	2	2
Taxes	1	1
None	3	1
Don't know/Refused	6	3

Source: Drawn from "Election 2004 Updated, Unmarried women. Unmarried women vote for change and strongly supported John Kerry," by Anna Greenberg and Jennifer Berktold, (Washington, D.C. Greenberg, Quinlan, Rosner Research Inc.) November 22, 2004.

The Democratic response to the 2006 State of the Union also showed some learning on the part of the Democrats. As mentioned earlier, the response was delivered by the newly elected Governor of Virginia, Tim Kaine. His campaign was notable for many successes, among them that he stuck to his anti-death penalty beliefs in a very conservative state out of his personal and religious convictions. In this instance, the messenger was a man of personal integrity and morality.

It seems simple to say that Democrats should pay attention to the personal attributes of their spokesmen and women. On the other hand, given the substantial achievements of say a Clinton or a Kennedy, Democrats want to trumpet those eras and those achievements. But it is difficult to do without also calling up the memories of the moral failings of the man. Just ask Al Gore.

Get right with God.

Democrats have to deal with religious voters. In the minds of too many voters Republicans are the pro-religion party and Democrats the anti-religion party. One friend of mine went canvassing in West Virginia during the 2004 election and was told more than once that if elected, Democrats would ban the Bible.

The perception that Democrats are the anti-religion Party is of recent historic vintage. It cannot be fully explained by the strength of the Evangelical vote even though the numbers of Evangelicals have grown in the past few years. Republican strength among Evangelical voters was substantial in the 1988 election. What is new is Republican strength among *all* churchgoers, not just Evangelicals. In 1988 Michael Dukakis fared only two points worse among regular churchgoers than did Bush.[17] But by the 2004 election regular churchgoers of all religious persuasions were more likely to vote Republican and those who rarely or never went to church were more likely to vote Democratic.[18]

How did this happen? It is, in part, of course, a reflection of a serious and well implemented Republican effort to court religious people of all persuasions, not just Evangelicals. But it is also a reflection of the fact that the base of the Democratic Party is made up, in part, of rabid secularists whose suspicion of religion and rightful distrust of its intrusion into democratic governance often comes off as hostility to religion. A disproportionate number of these people live in New York and Los Angeles and form the financial base of the Democratic Party. These extremely wealthy individuals are often drawn to politics by their support for controversial social issues such as abortion and gay marriage.

The solution to this problem is not, I repeat *not*, to reverse Democratic support on social issues like abortion and gay rights. However, there is no reason why Democrats shouldn't work as hard as Republicans have for the support of religious people. In addition to the hot button social issues, religious people also care deeply about the poor and in recent years many religious people see environmental protection as consistent with their religious beliefs. Note, for instance, formation of National Religious Partnership for the Environment which created the anti-SUV campaign called—"What would Jesus drive?"[19] Democrats have a lot to say to those of faith and yet more often than not, their language seems to have been honed in Hollywood and not in the pulpit.

In the future Democrats will find it easier to talk to religious people in ways that appeal to them because of a wholly unrelated development—the coming of age of the Internet in politics. The Institute for Politics, Democracy and the Internet has published a comprehensive study of large and small donors to the 2004 presidential campaign.[20] In that year more people contributed to politics than ever before and small contributions (less than $200) increased by 15 percent among Republicans and by 17 percent among Democrats—from the 2000 cycle, due to the ease of giving and the amount of information on the Internet.[21] The overall conclusion of the study, which compared big donors to small donors was that the new small donors were no more extreme than other donors and that, contrary to some popular wisdom, the introduction of small donors via the Internet was not having an additional polarizing effect on our politics.

But for our narrower purposes in this article there is one significant difference. Democratic small donors were more religious than Democratic big donors. Small donors were more than twice as likely as big donors to attend church once a week (33 percent to 13 percent) and they were more likely than big donors to say that religion is very important in their lives (26 percent to 17 percent).[22]

The growing power of small donors on the Democratic Party will decrease the power of the big donors and make it easier for Democrats to adopt policies and stances that appeal to religious voters. Two small examples from the 2000 presidential election illustrate this point. In 1999 Vice President Gore came out in favor of the use of federal funds for faith based social services. Overall the speech at a Salvation Army center in Atlanta was well received. But before that speech intense internal opposition came from the Party's financial base. Given that Gore was a sitting Vice President with a comfortable lead for the nomination the pressure was withstood—but it is doubtful that a lesser-known candidate, more dependent on the big "bundlers" could have done the same. Later, in the summer of 2000, the author was charged with supervising the writing of that year's Democratic platform. Language critical of the role of Hollywood and television in the shaping of children's views of the world, a particular interest of the Vice Presidential candidate Senator Joe Lieberman, was included in the platform. The author received numerous calls from Hollywood politicos threatening to pull back needed money. The language stayed but the pressure was real and blatant.

To the extent that future Democratic aspirants for President are less dependent on a cultural and financial elite—the better. It will allow them to speak to religious people on issues consistent with long time Democratic policies without the implicit or explicit threat of blackmail from their financial base.

Conclusion

The Democratic Party has a future that is both consistent with its past and yet adapted to the future. Changes in the reality of the American economy and changes in the base of the Party offer opportunities for Democrats to seize the initiative and appeal to a broader base. The failure of the Bush foreign policy provides an opportunity for a robust alternative, changes in the economy allow for the creation of a 21st century social safety net and changes in the base of the party mean that its candidates may be freer to attract those who have been turned off in the past.

Roundtable Discussion

Peter Beinart: What strikes me most about Elaine's very good paper is how uncontroversial her five points are in the Democratic Party today, and I think that says something about where the party is. It seems to me that if you took those five points and put them out there, you could get everybody, probably from Ted Kennedy—well, maybe not Ted Kennedy, since he's attacked by name, but everybody from Barbara Boxer to Tim Roemer, to agree—everybody in the Democratic Party basically united against Social Security privatization. Virtually everybody believes in some form you need universal healthcare. All the candidates in 2004 did. It was just a technical debate about how you got there. But everybody also believes that you need to be more pro-business and not go back to the at least perceived kind of politics of the 1960s and '70s on economic issues.

Everybody is very excited about peppering their speeches with references to the Bible. It seems to me it's become a kind of an epidemic in the Democratic Party. I worry a little bit that people who haven't actually read the Bible, probably shouldn't pepper their speeches with quotation from the Bible, because someone from the audience might actually ask them a question, and expect they know something about it.

I think everybody feels the Democratic Party needs to be stronger on foreign policy, and certainly everybody believes the Bush Administration is incompetent and should be held responsible. And it seems to me that the irony, I think, is that the Democratic Party is always attacked as being not unified, and it seems to me the problem the Democratic Party has, I think most of all, probably is that it's too unified. Or, put another way, it's not having the kind of serious ideological debates that you want to have a couple of years before a Presidential election to start clarifying things, so then candidates can run on them. It seems to me the model for this is Elaine and Bill Galston and their work between 1989 and 1991, where they went out and said some very, very controversial things that got some people very, very upset, but really broke taboos in the party, and then allowed a master politician like Bill Clinton to take some of those ideas and bring people back together, but in a place that was very different in 1992 than where they had been in 1988.

I worry that the problem with the Democratic Party is that the party is too united and is not actually having the kind of fundamental kind of sacred cow slaying debates that you need to at this point in a presidential cycle. As someone who, myself, has tried to spur those a little bit, I think that what's happened is that many people, including myself, thought that the post-2004 period would be a re-fight of the kind of DLC (Democratic Leadership Council) versus Rainbow Coalition fights of the 1980s. It turns out, in fact, that the DLC is no longer the DLC and the netroots that have emerged on the blogosphere are not the Rainbow Coalition. The DLC doesn't have the same Southern conservative flavor— if you look at the kind of politicians coming out of the South today—the John Edwards and Mark Warners—they are really not like the Sam Nunns and Chuck Robbs of a generation ago. The ideological distance from the center of the Democratic Party is much less. This is partly just because the Democratic Party has so few politicians in the South anymore, so they don't have that broad an ideological spectrum.

The DLC was against Social Security privatization. Even on trade, it seemed to me by the end of the Clinton Administration, the DLC and the unions were coming together to a certain view that supported trade deals with real labor and environmental protections.

And the netroots, who many people assumed were the next coming of Jesse Jackson—the kind of hard left in the Democratic Party, thinking about web sites like *Daily Kos*—have turned out to be something different. If you read the new book by the founder of *Daily Kos* and another influential blog, *mydd.com*, what you see is explicitly non-ideological. They basically say that they don't really care what the ideas are. They assume Democrats pretty much agree on most things, anyway. And they're only interested in tactics. And the truth is, when *moveon.org,* which is considered the hard left in the Democratic Party, and did a poll amongst its members for what ad they should run during the Super Bowl, the one that won was a deficit reduction ad.

It's true that there are currents, of course, of cultural liberalism and to some degree, dovish foreign policy in the Democratic Party, but I think it is a mistake to see the activists today as the same as the activists of the 80s. The activists today—a lot of those people are very excited about Mark Warner, for instance. If the DLC is not the DLC, they are really not the second coming of the Rainbow Coalition. So the problem, it seems to me, with all of this—with all of this unity—is that the party is not having the kinds of debates that it should be having—the kind of fundamental debates about what the Democrats believe. And it seems to me that if they don't have those debates, you could have a situation in 2008, a little akin to 2004, where no candidate really (except for to some degree, John Edwards) had a message that sounded like he was describing the real problems that Americans face, and he had a narrative for talking about it.

So let me just end by talking about what it seems to me some of those debates the Democrats should be screaming about with one another are:

The first and most important is to reprise the debate of the 1980s about globalization, which is to say, I think the Democratic Party needs some very strong voices saying, as people like Robert Kuttner did, for instance, in 1980 that the Robert Reich model, which is basically where we're pro-free trade, we're pretty pro-liberal immigration, but we can do certain kinds of things at home to allow people to adjust, particularly people without college degrees, allowing them to adjust so they can survive in this new economy. I think that argument needs to be taken on in the Democratic Party again, because I don't think the Democratic Party base has actually been sold on it. I'm not necessarily saying it's my position, but I think the debate desperately needs to be had, because there are so many people, not only in the Democratic Party, but particularly the base of the Democratic Party, who don't believe that anymore, and that's part of the reason the Democratic Party in Congress doesn't have anyone who votes for free trade anymore.

I think somebody should come out and make the kind of argument that Dick Gephardt was making in 1988. That should force the kind of mainstream establishment of the party, the kind of Robert Reich wing of the party. Or you could say the Robert Rubin wing of the party, to respond with much, much harder, more serious, more radical thinking about what you actually are going to do in terms of domestic policy if you're still going to have a pro-free trade, relatively pro-immigration stance, so that working-class Americans don't see their standards of living decline.

I think Elaine is right. Healthcare is a very important part of it, but a much broader conception, I think of social insurance is going to be necessary. That argument is going to have to be made if the Democratic Party is going to sustain a pro-free trade and a relatively pro-free immigration position. Just a little bit more money for job retraining here and there, I think, is not going to cut it.

The second debate is that there is a fundamental divide between the Democratic Party's establishment and its base about whether it believes that there is a war on terror. What the polling shows is not that the Democrats are necessarily isolationists per se, but that they do not see the war on terror as their prism for seeing the world, whereas I think many people in the Washington foreign policy establishment of the Democratic Party still do. That debate needs to be had, and the secondary debate that needs to be had is whether Democrats believe that democracy promotion should be America's number one priority in the world. It seems to be there is a position, a kind of a Tony Blair position, which says that the war on terror is the biggest deal around, and that democracy promotion is the right answer, but we need to do it from a much stronger international institution. This is the kind of thing that Bill Clinton and Tony Blair were talking about on the way to the Kosovo War. There is a very different position, focused around things like energy independence, homeland security, the kind of stuff that you saw coming out of Congress in the Real Security plan the Democrats came out with, which is much less about transforming the world, and much more about protecting America from the world—much more realist—much less Wilsonian. That debate, it seems to me, is not really happening in the Democratic Party.

The last point I would make is that I think there needs to be a reprise of the debates that Bill Clinton talked about very well about how to bring the country together with a greater sense of community. It seems to me that Bill Clinton was so masterful with his famous speech in the Macomb County, and then his speech in Detroit, in creating a sense in a country that was very divided over race, that we were one country and that we had values that transcended that. It seems to me the challenge for the next generation of Democrats will be to do the same thing around the questions of immigration, where the country is clearly (Pat Caddell and I were talking about this last night) potentially divided about its sense of who is American, and also about this question of red state and blue state. That's part of the reason that Barack Obama's speech touched such a chord in 2004, and there is a very powerful place for some politician who can find the language of talking about what unites us as Americans because of the fear, not along racial lines anymore, but along cultural, religious, and ethnic lines that we are becoming too divided again. So it seems to me those would be debates that one would want to see happening in the Democratic Party, and if that they have people yelling at one another a bit, I think that would be a sign of progress. Thanks.

Patrick Caddell: All right. Let me first of all pour some cold water on a lot of this discussion. First of all, I'm listed as a political consultant. That's only because no one knows what to call me, because I used to be one. Now I'm a born again virgin, politically, and don't have these problems of history. I want to start by saying I agree (and have for a long time) with a lot of what Elaine was writing and saying about the practical problems of the party, and what Peter was saying and what others will say. But let me start out with a fundamental dissent, which is only when the Democratic Party once again becomes a party, once again has some moral fundamental beliefs other than, "My God, we're desperate to be in office again, and God, give us the silver bullet that will win," then it might actually succeed. I think it might win this year, despite that. I think actually not having George Bush and the Republican Party may suffice. If it doesn't, by the way, then you might as well close up the shop, because if you cannot win in this election year, with everything going for you, it tells you that you're fundamentally defective, and the Democratic Party truly is fundamentally defective.

I will deal with that on one issue to start with, which is NAFTA (the North American Free Trade Agreement), which I totally dissent from. And what Elaine and what Peter were saying about being the pro-business party—how can you be the party of basically what is capital corruption—and I'm not talking about the 1930s and the 1960s. I'm a big capitalist. I think what this country really needs is a good dose of what it believes in: Free enterprise, which it doesn't have now. You have both political parties auctioned off and bought on behalf of special interests. The price paid for ordinary Americans is enormous. And the price paid for this country is enormous. And no one will speak about it.

I'll give you an example of this. In 2004, during the middle of the campaign, we have a whole series of scandals coming about, how all of the Mutual Funds in New York and Wall Street have been cheating and stealing from their own customers for years. Not one of this would you hear from the candidate of the Democratic Party, John Kerry, or from its candidates, and the reason is very simple—how can you when you, in fact, are the candidate of those people? John Kerry's function on the Finance Committee was essentially (when he served on the Banking Committee) to serve as a Democratic messenger boy for Wall Street. And this goes back, fundamentally, to Bill Clinton, who destroyed, I believe, hollowed out the soul of the Democratic Party, both on a moral basis and also on a political basis, by running the Democratic Party to Wall Street. You cannot have two election cycles when you have the Democratic Party's chief number one source of money being Wall Street and financial institutions and tell me that you have a Democratic Party that cares about ordinary people. Now we're told, "Well, look at how great it was in the 1990s for people because of the booming economy." Yes, with two time bombs—the six trillion dollars that would blow up when the bubble blew up that came out of ordinary Americans'

401Ks, because of the criminal activity in Wall Street and the other areas, and the fact that basically, Democrats sell out.

I'll give you an example from this very year. The bankruptcy bill tells you everything you need to know. There was no great clamoring in the election year of 2004 to have a bankruptcy bill—to go out and make sure that people could not get a free start to take care of the credit card companies and the banks. But who led that fight? None other than Hillary Clinton, Charles Schumer, Joe Biden, Chris Dodd, and other people; some of them are close friends of mine—or have been. The reason they did it is because that's who owns them. Now, let's get specific about that. In the year 2000, when the Bankruptcy Court Reform came up, it was eventually vetoed by President Clinton. I watched this with some fascination because I watching Bill Moyer interview, I'm sorry, I can't remember her name. She and her daughter did a wonderful book on the two-family income trap, talking about she met with Hillary Clinton at Hillary Clinton's request in Cambridge in 2000, and she was talking about bankruptcy, and she explained what it did to ordinary people. Hillary Clinton was horrified and went home and supposedly convinced her husband to veto the bill. Now she gets to the United States Senate and as a candidate of Wall Street, basically, she's the one leading the fight for it. When you no longer stand for your own people and are mouthing the words saying, "We're for ordinary people, but we're not for big business," when you are, there's no competition in the political system.

And let me start by saying that this is not about class. That's all Democrats know how to talk about—rich people, poor people—no, it's about criminals, it's about right and wrong, it's about what is morally justified, and until the Democratic Party can stand up for what it believes in, it will go nowhere. It may win an election or two, but right now that is its problem, and you can see it in a series of examples, and I will show you. Yesterday you could watch as I did, yesterday morning, the debate at C-SPAN in the House in defense of 527s, watching liberal Democrats who supposedly are for campaign finance reform, talking about free speech like they were the Club for Growth and money. That is basically having whored themselves to big money, they do not know how to disengage from it. And I believe what Peter said and what Elaine said is right. The whole future of this is small donors. And it goes to the fact that these people actually do want to have something to believe in.

And let me just say this about the war foreign policy: The Democratic Party, I feel, live in fear of one thing, that someone will take what I saw that was run on Fox by Sean Hannity, and I was there when he did it on the show, after January of 2005, when the Iraqis were voting and everyone was amazed. People were running around with their purple fingers, being shot at to vote—an interesting idea—and the Democrats put together statements leading right up to that Sunday vote with John Kerry, Howard Dean, Ted Kennedy, and others, which you could not look at without turning your face feeling they were rooting for us to lose. They were rooting for America to lose. It's the body language, and the answer is again, political victory no matter what the cost. It comes across this way, and that's why the Democrats look so incompetent in Washington, because they stand for nothing.

Let me give you an example. We forget that between the years 2001 and 2003 it was a Democratic Senate, for the most part. When George Bush went to West Point—I used to be on the board at West Point, so it was something I was quite keenly interested in—and gave his speech announcing the policy of pre-emption attack, or as I call it the wolf with madness, being turned into national policy. Do you know how many hearings Joe Biden and John Kerry and the Senate Foreign Relations Committee had on that change of national policy? Zero! You look at the question about the defense and what happened with the post invasion, which you find is the lack of really exposing the fact that this administration had no policies, and in fact, was in the hands of some very well-meaning bright people, with in fact, insane foreign policy positions. No hearings on this. Nothing would make us "look weak." So what we do is look weak, and do nothing in the interim, either. And you can see this again and again.

My favorite is the PATRIOT Act. And I didn't know about this until I was reading it in the *Newsweek* excerpt of Steve Brill's book, *After*, which proves that nobody, by the way, reads news magazines. I've never found anybody who also read it. But I'm reading a book excerpt, and one of the things it's covering is developing of the PATRIOT Act. Now in the House, when the administration came up with that bill, the revolt among Republican conservative libertarians and the ACLU (American Civil Liberties Union) types was overwhelming. A bill came out of the House by the same Judiciary Committee that we all watched during the Bill Clinton impeachment—totally divided—they came out unanimous. And it scaled back the request of John Ashcroft and the administration. In conference committee almost all of those scale-backs were restored. They were restored by Democrats under the leadership of Tom Daschle, who announced in a caucus, "We're going to do this, because we will then look tough if we give them everything they want," which led to the vote of [Senator Russ] Feingold against the bill—the only person. And I looked at that. I fell off my chair, almost literally. I had no idea that that's how the Democrats had come to the position they had come to on the PATRIOT Act. It all goes back to the same thing—you cannot run around and contrive yourself on every issue and never stand for anything.

Let me just say this: The American people right now are in an uproar. They are willing, in a sense, I would think, to overthrow both of these parties. As was said before me, this country is not fiercely divided red and blue. The elites are, the political activists are, but not the country. But what you have are two corrupted political parties. But let me end on this: When the Republican Party corrupts itself, at least it does so in the service of a philosophy it believes in. When the Democrats corrupt themselves, they destroy everything they believe in. And that is what is killing the Democratic Party. All you have to look at is the corruption in this state of California, which is a Democratic state and is the most corrupt state in America—and I'm glad to defend that proposition—but until the party faces up to believing in something (and I also agree with Elaine), and also believing in moral values, which gets you back on the right side of God, then it will face the fate of either being taken over or disappearing. Thank you.

Nelson Polsby: I'm going to try doing this sitting down. Elaine's been making sense to me for I don't know, how long has it been?

Elaine Kamarck: I don't know—since 1976?

Polsby: Anyway, I liked your paper very much, because it seemed to me there were really only two points I want to make about it. A lot of the rhetoric you hear about advice to the Democratic Party begins by invoking Newt Gingrich's Contract with America as the model, the way to go, which perpetrates the myth that anybody knew or cared about the Contract with America. They didn't. What is the case is that we have a tendency in talking generally about the two parties to turn them into twins when, in fact, they are quite different in the way in which they are constituted.

Republicans do philosophy. The Democrats really don't. Calls for the Democrats to do philosophy like good Republicans is just simply a waste of time in my view. Democrats are unified, not by philosophy, but by bargains. It's also the case that we have a compound Constitution. The idea that you can have a unified opposition when you have a disunified structure of government seems to me sort of highly utopian. You can have a unified opposition only, if basically you give up a lot of territory that there is no reason in the world for Democrats to give up at this stage of the game. So Elaine's basic number one point, go left, go right, is absolutely right. It responds to (a) the way Democrats are, and (b) the way the Constitution requires you to exploit the political opportunity, which the Bush Administration is handing them. Okay, that's my main point.

My second point has to do with a very smart idea that Elaine had, which she talked about in the paper, which unfortunately, won't work. It is to notice that pensions are killing the U.S. industrial sector and the Democratic Party can make hay by basically socializing pensions, taking pensions and responsibility for pensions away from the private sector (the industrial sector, particularly). I think it probably makes very good economic sense. It makes no political sense at all, because business men who will benefit from this will not be grateful. The reason I think so, is because I know something about—we all know something about—the way doctors faced Medicare. It was all perfectly clear that Medicare was going to be a bonanza for the medical profession. They opposed it, anyway. I think this basically is the same problem. Maybe in a way it validates some of the things underlying Pat's analysis when he says in effect that Democrats can be bribed, Republicans can't. That's right. I think I'll let Ruy do the rest. Thanks.

Ruy Teixeira: Elaine has put five points into play, and I guess I largely agree with Peter. I think what's interesting about them is that they're not particularly controversial at this point. I guess I would also see a couple of big problems with them. One is that, as points, they are really more approaches or very general recommendations. I'm not sure they have enough specificity to them to be really that useful in terms of guiding Democratic strategy. The second big problem I see is that they are only ideas. Let me explain that.

In terms of the ideas not being specific enough, and maybe not having enough content to them, Elaine recommends we *go left and right on domestic policy*. It's certainly clear enough what going to the left means—universal healthcare, do something about pensions, fill in your favorite domestic program there. But then she says go right in terms of having a radical pro-growth policy. I just don't know what that means, other than she recommended doing something about corporate taxes. Again, just what the content of a radical pro-growth policy is that's really different from where Democrats have come from in the past definitely needs some filling in.

Give competence another try. Obviously the Democrats are going to run on being competent, because there is widespread feeling that Republicans are not. But the specific recommendation is to take FEMA out of DHS. Again, while this is probably a pretty good idea, it doesn't seem to have the overarching and compelling nature of a program in this area, or a short set of recommendations. I just don't see this as really grabbing people.

Get a coherent foreign policy. I think all Democrats agree with that at this point, but what's a modern view of national security, as she says at one point in her paper, that includes environmental and health degradation? She also says spend more money on the military and intelligence assets and be willing to use military force. All of this is basically pretty vague. I think most Democrats would say yeah, we probably need to spend some more money, but where? We need to be willing to use military force, but where, and under what circumstances?

And what's left out of here is quite striking: what to do about Iraq? I think this is the question of the moment. This is what people are thinking about. Democrats, if they are going to project a coherent foreign policy, have to have a coherent answer on what to do about Iraq, and what to do after we pull out, if we do pull out, and so on. That's not provided here, and it's something I think Democrats are going to have to think about.

The idea of *having a better messenger* is sort of hard to argue with, but who? Are we talking then *not* about Hillary Clinton? If so, who? We need to fill in the specifics of who these good messengers are, and won't have us excusing bad behavior with good policy.

And finally, *getting right with God*, appealing to religious voters. Again, this is something that is very difficult to argue with, but it's also very difficult to explain exactly how to do it. How do you appeal to religious voters, and which religious voters, and on what basis? She seems to recommend a sort of social Christianity type of approach, and there is some evidence of some splits among more religious voters on some of these issues, but again, it's not exactly clear how to pursue that. It's something that is going to have to be filled in quite a lot to be all that useful. Also, I think there is a certain defensive quality to the way it's put forward. You also see this in the long paper she did with Bill Galston, *The Politics of Polarization*. This is a little bit of a return to "the politics of inoculation," where Democrats seek to reassure swing voters, moderates, and independents that, in fact, they're really not that bad. Message—we're religious. Message—we don't condone bad behavior. Message—we think foreign policy is important. Again, I think the content has to be clear. It has to be clear what exactly—as Pat was saying—you stand for. I'm not so sure these ideas really do the trick.

The second big problem I see is that, even if they were better and clearer ideas than they are—and I think that's something we're all trying to work on—would they be enough by themselves? Is all we need: better ideas? I think the answer to that is, "No." Consider the book that has already been mentioned by Peter, *Crashing the Gate*, by Markos Moulitsas and Jerome Armstrong of the two leading Democratic-oriented blogs, *Daily Kos* and *MyDD*. That book—which I recommend to you—is primarily about how the Democrats need to be better as an *organization*. As an organization, they need to be better, smarter, and tougher. They need smarter ads, they need to take advantage of new media, they need smarter, fresher consultants and they need to let the market speak when consultants lose and advice is bad. Such consultants should be punished and you shouldn't keep shoveling money at them.

You also need to have a stronger party in more places. The Democratic Party in many places is just kind of a shell. You need a fifty-state strategy; you've got to compete everywhere. To hell, they argue, with interest groups that veto or try to veto viable Democratic candidates in places like Rhode Island and Pennsylvania. For example, Jim Langevin would possibly have been the strongest Senatorial candidate to knock off Lincoln Chaffee in Rhode Island, but he got vetoed by NARAL (National Abortion Rights Action League) and didn't wind up running. They've also raised problems about Bob Casey in Pennsylvania who was the obvious guy to beat Santorum and so on. It's just something that happens over and over again. Whenever you get a bunch of Democrats in a room, they tend to push their favorite issue. Interest groups tend to be very parochial about what they're willing to support. Play to win at all times is a better approach.

So, don't let things like interest groups get in the way. And, very near and dear to Armstrong's and Moulitsas' hearts, unleash the netroots. Unleash this new social force that's represented by the blogs and by all the small donors who put money into campaigns over the Internet (which is one way of counterbalancing the big money that Pat and Elaine were talking about). Unleashing the net roots is key. This is a social force that is going to very much be a critical part of what the Democratic Party is going to be in the future, and the Democratic Party has to be reoriented, restructured—the money changers have to be thrown out of the temple, as it were. If you don't do that—even if you had better ideas—the Democratic Party won't be able to effectively deliver those ideas and do it in a way that will allow them to actually win, which is the goal of a good strategy.

Okay, so I think it's pretty clear what Democrats need. They need better, clearer ideas *and* they need better, smarter organization of the party and message delivery. You have to do both things, I think. If the Democrats could do that, they'd be in a lot better shape. Well, how do you do that? How can you get there from here? I offer two tests to focus Democrats' thinking about how to do this and to provoke more debate. I think Peter's absolutely right: these are hard things to figure out. If Democrats are pretending they've got them all figured out, that's not good You need as much debate as possible to clarify these things.

The first test I'd recommend is what I call the white working class test. The Democrats in many ways have a burgeoning coalition. Overall, the country and its demographics are changing, as I explained in my book with John Judis, *The Emerging Democratic Majority,* in ways that are pretty favorable, on net, to the Democrats. Of course, that could be debated, but what's not debatable, is that, if Democrats lose white working class voters—defined here as white non-college voters—by as large margins as they typically have been doing, it doesn't matter if you have a burgeoning coalition. It doesn't matter if the demographics of the country are in many ways shifting in your favor. In 2004, the Democrats lost the white working class vote on the presidential election by twenty-three points. You see margins similar to that in a lot of state-wide races, particularly in the more contested states. This is really how the Republicans have built their rather thin majority coalition—through gaining supermajorities of the white working class vote, especially components of that vote like married women.

So the test would be: How are Democrats' ideas going to be received by moderate and independent white working class voters?—the more accessible members of that group. Will those ideas really capture their imaginations? Will those ideas make clear to them what Democrats stand for? Will those ideas really move them? I think that's extremely important to think about. And, related to this, can you *deliver* your message to these voters? Do you know how to get to these voters in exurbia? Do you know how to get to these voters in rural areas? Do you know how to get to those voters in small and medium-size metro areas around the country? That's where the Democrats are getting killed, so can you deliver your message to those voters in those kinds of places? That's a lot where I think the Markos/Jerome kind of thing about a new reform party that gets beyond the establishment in Washington can be so important.

The second test I propose is the back of an envelope test. Your ideas as you project them, do they go back to and reinforce a set of, say, four principles that can be put on the back of an envelope? Do they really help define the Democrats? Will these ideas help people realize who the Democrats are and what they stand for? I call that "the politics of definition", and I think that's going to be, in the end, much more effective for the Democrats than the politics of inoculation, which is some of where Elaine is coming from. Certainly it's been a strategy in the past with the DLC, which practices the most orthodox form of the politics of inoculation. The politics of definition is also a better approach than "the politics of mobilization", which essentially says: let's just get the base out; let's crank up the rhetoric and make sure we get as many of our friends riled up as we can. I think what the Democrats are going to need to do is *define* themselves, and I think you can't really define yourselves unless you get back to core principles.

Let's look at the Republicans' core principles. They're pretty simple, or at least that's the way most people think about them. If you ask the person on the street what Republicans stand for they might say low taxes, small government, strong defense and family values. That's great! You've only taken up half the envelope so that's definitely a point in their favor. Now at this point the Republicans have a slight problem in that those things are no longer coming through as clearly to voters as they once did. Now Republicans appear to stand for a free lunch, broken corrupt government, stupid defense, and the sort of global adventures that don't seem to work out, not to mention social extremism and intolerance. There's a lot of things that have gone wrong with the way that Republicans are trying to project their image around their core principles.

So the Democrats need to flip that and make it clear to people what *their* core principles are and what they stand for and promote ideas that connect to them correctly. Some things that occurred to me are: instead of a free lunch you get what you pay for; instead of broken government, government that works (as Elaine also talked about); instead of stupid defense that gets us involved in adventures that don't work out, smart, effective defense; instead of social extremism, strong families, social tolerance and middle class opportunity. In fact, I wrote a paper with Jacob Hacker where we argue that Democrats should focus their economic program around *providing security to expand opportunity*. What Americans really want is to get ahead. So if Democrats can project they are for strong families *that can get ahead*, they might be onto something.

Now, of course, I've probably taken up an envelope and a half, so this needs work. But I think this is the right idea. All of your ideas should get back to a small set of principles that people can ID the Democrats with and know what they stand for. So, when you vote for a Democrat, that's what you're voting for. You're voting for those core principles and that's what you expect them to do in office. That makes your vote a lot clearer and more meaningful that it was before. I think in the end that would help the Democrats solve their white working class problem, as well as adding to their burgeoning coalition and, in the end, could be an effective strategy both for winning *and* for governance. Other people may disagree, but those are my ideas. Thank you!

Kamarck: Let me start with just two short comments. One is I think the politics of inoculation are sort of an inevitable part of American political parties. Compassionate conservatism was part of the politics of inoculation. I mean, I just think that when you have a two-party system and particularly in this day and age when you're very closely matched in the electorate, it's not very ideologically satisfying, but I think that's what both political parties end up having to do.

Secondly, on the business side, let me just say I actually agree with a lot of what Pat has said on this, but I take it one step further. The impact of special interests, money on politics, has created a vast distortion of capitalism. In other words, what happens now is there are enormous government subsidies to certain kinds of industry. That bleeds tax dollars from certain sectors that ought to be going into programs that create innovation, programs that do R and D, programs that in fact are pro-growth programs. So, in fact, I see an opportunity for Democrats to be more free market than Republicans by frankly taking on this enormous mess of special interest tax breaks, weaning certain portions of the economy. Let's start with the oil and gas—weaning them off the government teat, and using that money to do actual kinds of investments that create jobs that create innovation, etc.

Patrick's right. The reason we have this mess is that both the Democratic and Republican politicians over the years have gotten addicted to various special interest money. I would just take that one step further and say that is a distortion of a free market. It is hurting capitalism, and Democrats ought to be pro-capitalist economy, and the more pro-capitalist you are, the more you also then have to argue for a strong and secure social safety net. Go any place in the world (particularly Eastern Europe and Russia) that are emerging and trying to emerge into a capitalist society. And what you find is, do you know what they really, really need? They need a social safety net, because you frankly can't have one without the other, so that's kind of the gist of my going right and going left simultaneously.

Caddell: Let me just say, Elaine, I tend to agree with you. I mean, I think the issue here is when the most radical magazine in America is *Fortune* Magazine. It's not in the *New Republic* where you see arguments against what are essentially corporate corruption, corporate socialization, and so forth. It's in *Fortune* Magazine, which has a cover story. You see the *Fortune* Magazine cover put these people in jail—a year before the Enron scandal—but you don't hear that from any Democrats, and the reason is what Elaine says, which is that corporate socialism is killing this country.

The oil industry—I saw yesterday where they had a report where the former president of Exxon said that 40 percent of costs that are happening in gasoline is being cranked up by the speculators gambling around and driving up the price. Now you tell me government can't do something about that game? The same way you can deal with gambling? Of course you can. The fact of the matter is you can be pro-business sense or pro what I call free enterprise, as opposed to capitalism. And that Democrats haven't stood for. There's one thing other I don't agree on about the interest groups: As long as the Democratic Party has to kneel down and pay service to NARAL, every time voters see Democrats defending things that are indefensible, such as abortions in the ninth month and other things which it seems to look like it supports—it will never move on social values. You cannot be hostage to a set of interest groups. If they want to have a political party let them have one. But you have to have some principles to stand for, and you cannot have to go, like a bunch of Democratic candidates do all the time, to these conferences and reduce themselves to puppets. It does a lot to knock out the idea of strong leadership.

Uh, well, so much for the Democratic Party.

Question: Let me pose a question to the panel: What can the Democrats of 2006 learn from 1994—Nelson alluded to this, that the contract itself was not a major cause of the shift of 1994, but if not, what was, and is there anything the Democrats can learn from that?

Polsby: Well, what happened in '94, it seems to me, is a whole bunch of toxic material built up in the system, and the Democrats got hurt by most of all, I think, the House bank scandal, which was a complete and utter phony from beginning to end. Nevertheless, that's what did it, and thereafter people said, well, it was the Contract with America, which it wasn't.

Caddell: I totally agree with you on the Contract with America—I saw the polls and not 10 percent of the people even knew what it was or even heard about it. I remember, I was doing an interview right after the election when Connie Brooker was doing a piece on Newt Gingrich—a kind of coming to power piece, and I said, "You know, these people will destroy themselves," which they quickly did when shutting down the government, because they actually believed that they got an endorsement for ideological extremism. What they got endorsed for was what Nelson said, which is that this was a toxic political system, and it was time to deal with a lot of these problems, and because of the unpopularity of Bill Clinton. The worst thing is that the Republicans believed it themselves, which led to the fact that they managed to get elected a man who, at that moment, was a walking politically dead Bill Clinton.

Kamarck: Let me just add to that. I think there have been three incredible teaching moments as we call them in American politics recently, which Democrats ought to take more advantage of and which Republicans have been hurt by.

The first one was the government shutdown. What was stunning about that was all sorts of people in America suddenly realized that yeah, they didn't know what the federal government did, but it affected absolutely everything, right down to Catholic charities, which had to shut its doors because so much of its money came from the federal government—so suddenly, this big behemoth was not a distant thing that just took your tax dollars. It was everywhere.

The second teaching moment, of course, was 9-11, where we saw it was public servants, it was civil servants who were going into those buildings and dying and being heroes.

And I think the third teaching moment was Katrina. Nobody in their right mind thinks that the private sector could have rescued New Orleans. Okay? Sometimes you simply do need the government, and you do need it to work. And the interesting thing to me about the contract with America is that the substance of that contract was also dead within twelve months. I mean, I know, because one of the things I fought in the White House was, we fought to preserve OSHA—the Occupational Safety and Health Administration, which was target numero uno of the Contract of America, and you know what? We did some reforms there—in fact, we used it on the Democratic side. We used it, you know, as pressure to push reforms, but the fact of the matter is, OSHA is still alive and well, as are all the regulatory apparatus that the Contract of America attacked. I think there is a new appreciation for the fact that yeah, sometimes you really do need the government to work.

Teixeira: The Democratic situation this year can be summed up by looking at the macro and micro environment. If you look at macro indicators—right direction/wrong track, presidential approval ratings, and a variety of other things—this is a very unfavorable environment for the Republicans and they should lose lots of seats. So standard forecasting model might predict that based on these national indicators, Republicans should lose something like thirty to thirty-five seats—a big shift in the Democrats' favor.

The problem is, if you look at the micro environment and evaluate these things on a race-by-race basis, it's hard to see where those shifts come from. You might see only eight or nine seats lost by the Republicans. That's because of the advantages of incumbency, the location of contested open seats and a variety of very specific factors having to do with the 435 individual House races and 33 Senate races.

So the issue for the Democrats, taking a lesson from 1994—where the Republicans effectively nationalized the '94 election (and the Contract of America was only one part of that and probably not the most important part)—is how they can nationalize the election. That is, make it as much as they can about the Bush Administration and who's running the country as possible.

The second lesson is that if you've got a political wind at your back, you can pick up a lot of seats that you didn't actually think you had much of a chance of getting and therefore you need to contest as many races as possible. The most critical factor here is money. Your ability to come up with great challengers in each and every district that's even remotely contestable is limited, but one thing that research teaches us is that money can make up for a mediocre challenger. If these challengers have enough money to be competitive and there's a wind at their back in a nationalized election like 2006 may be, you'll wind up getting a lot of people over the finish line you might not have guessed could get there. But they can only do it with the adequate money.

Analyses suggest if you throw additional money at the difficult races—the ones that are not the standard thirty or forty seats the pundits say are contestable—those additional dollars are much more likely, in an expected valued sense, to produce additional gains for your party than throwing extra money into heavily-contested races, where that money has diminishing marginal returns. So stick that money on more long shots—more medium to long shots in a nationalized election like 2006 may be. That's how you could get the most juice out of this election.

Beinart: It strikes me that given what everyone has said and how much of an opportunity there is for a populist anti-Washington, anti-corruption message, it's striking to me that so far the Democratic Party really hasn't articulated that message very well or very coherently. I mean, there are a lot of challenges we've been talking about that are very difficult. This one seems actually, you know, easier. Republicans were able to do it in 1994, and they didn't have all of the gifts the Democrats have now. Democrats, in some ways, have much more have to work with than the Republicans had in 1994, and yet, there is not a kind of a Gingrich bomb-throwing figure who has emerged as someone who has kind of put out a message of anti-corruption anger. I think that's a question Democrats have to think about—about why that hasn't happened.

Polsby: I want to put an asterisk on that one unifying figure thing. That's Washington talking, folks. What they need is—out in the individual districts they need—people who are—yeah, and I think they have got them. The one unifying figure is journalistically convenient, but it's not necessary, not responsive to the actual way in which our system is organized.

Caddell: Let me agree with Nelson. I mean, this Washington myopia about what you need politically. What happened in '94 was, everything came to a head. You had Republican candidates out there. But, you know, here's what worries me about the Democrats, about '06. First of all, I agree with the problem gerrymandering has caused. The fact that the Democratic Party cannot stand and no political party will stand up and say the sovereignty of the American people and their democracy is absolute, and that the idea of depriving people of their sovereignty by gerrymandering is, in fact, worse than treason—tells you something about the weakness of the political process, because both sides are in this. I live in a state where there are no competitive elections, where a sixth of the nation lives and not one State Senate, one State Assembly seat or Congressional seat is competitive, because both parties get in the backroom and lock it up. And then when you have an argument to do something about it, every one of the groups in the Democratic Party fights as hard as it can against it on the notion the Democratic Party first, and democracy in America second. You know, sometime when somebody stands up in one of these parties for America first, it might actually win.

Secondly, look what's happening in Ohio. You have a Democratic candidate that runs in Cincinnati for a seat that he has no chance of winning, almost wins a special election, wants to run for the Senate, and is denied the candidacy because he is not the candidate of the Washington political establishment and will not serve as their lap boy, so he is displaced from running. You do that enough times, you will lose.

The third thing is—back on this thing about reform: The lobbying scandal. Look at the Democrats. I mentioned Chris Dodd yesterday. Rahm Emmanuel standing on the House floor. The man was the bagman for Bill Clinton and big business in the White House, getting up and talking about how we're going to run against corruption of the Republican Party, when the whole country knows the Democrats are equally corrupt. That is a problem. If you want to be a candidate against corruption, you must have a party that, in fact, reflects being against corruption.

Kamarck: Can I put one note in—this just reminded me of something that Ruy had said. One of the bright spots in this on the mobilization front is—and it also kind of picks up some of these Washington/anti-Washington themes that Pat's been bringing up. Howard Dean, the chairman of the Democratic Party, has been in a pitched battle with the leadership of the House and the Senate over simply the expenditure of the Democratic Party's money, and Dean believes that the purpose of a party chairman is to actually build the party in the states, and build them in all fifty states. There's just stuff happening here that's quite marvelous, and in Washington they hate it.

Let me give you a small example. The Democratic Party of North Dakota where we happen to have a Senator that we'd like to hang on to—and I think we probably will hang on to—that party as an organization, following the 2004 elections, had FEC problems it needed to solve, it was bankrupt, and it also had IRS problems. It needed a ton of just lawyering and accounting to get it to the point where it could even think about doing the stuff that a state political party is supposed to do. Well, what happened was the DNC (Democratic National Committee) sent them help. The lawyers, the accountants, and the full-time executive director paid, and in fact, that state party is now a party that can help re-elect a Democratic Senator, who otherwise should be vulnerable, and can do the things political parties are supposed to do. Lots of people came back from the field in 2004, saying, "Oh my God what a mess it was out there, because the parties were a mess." The fact of the matter is, you can't start fixing some of these sorts of just boring organizational, mundane problems, if you start fixing them in the spring of the Presidential election year. You don't have a capacity to do the kind of get-out-the-vote stuff. The Republicans have largely been immune to this, because traditionally they have hired executive directors for state parties from Washington, and they have watched carefully the health and the organizational capacity of their state parties. Dean is doing this. It is the great source of his strength. Those of us who know and care about parties think he's doing a terrific job. In Washington, however, he is getting nothing but grief, because they are looking at his cash on hand and saying, "Oh, no, you need to be giving more money directly to candidates," and he's saying, "I'm doing something that's helping candidates, but I'm building parties."

Question: Your presentations have been focused on the party in Washington. What about the grassroots activists and the power of the internet?

Teixeira: I did try to highlight somewhat the role of the grassroots/netroots and how critical that is. I think it's the case that the DCCC (Democratic Congressional Campaign Committee) is not nearly as experimental in trying to contest races as it probably should be and not willing to give these more marginal races a lot of money. So, while they've expanded the playing field a substantial amount from what they originally planned, a lot of the money for those marginal races is going to have to come from other places. I think the netroots are going to help provide a lot of that. My sense is a lot of money will be raised for a lot of relatively obscure races on the Internet this year, and I think it's going to wind up being very helpful, indeed.

Beinart: That's why I feel a lot of the complaining that is coming out of this panel is, in some ways, outdated. I mean, I think the truth of the matter is that things are changing quite rapidly. I mean, you saw in the '80s and '90s a shift in power from outsiders to insiders in the Democratic Party after the sense that the party had lost control in the '70s because too much power had been dispersed to activists through the McGovern Commission reforms. I think you've seen that pendulum switch back now, because of two factors: First of all, this incredible amount of energy that exists in the Democratic Party that has been provoked by George W. Bush and the war in Iraq, and secondly, the fact that those people now have a mechanism by which they can give money: the Internet. The Democratic Party is not a party of poor people. I mean, the Democratic Party—and you saw this in the Howard Dean campaign's fundraising. The Democratic Party has lots and lots and lots of people who can give a reasonable amount of money.

You know, it seems to me—if Hillary Clinton runs and loses it will be because it turns out that what you saw in the Howard Dean campaign was exponentially increased because of the continued arousal of grassroots activists and the power of the Internet, so that actually she gets out-raised by Russ Feingold or Al Gore. Remember before Howard Dean imploded, after Howard Dean raised all of that money, Washington came to him. Let's remember this. I mean, there was a period there when everyone was jumping over one another to get on the Howard Dean bandwagon, and then it turned out that he didn't actually have the support people thought he had. But people in Washington will move when it happens.

Caddell: I think you're on to a very important point. I think Ruy said it too, which is you have to deal with the fact that the power right now is in the grassroots. The movement that created Howard Dean—Howard Dean did not create that movement. That movement created him. Unfortunately, he wasn't up to the movement. The point is, it was very vibrant and very real, and it provided the resources of which the gentleman was just speaking. The question to the grassroots is are you going to put up with, like in this state, a corrupt Democratic Party essentially, or are you going to have some principles to stand for something other than hating George Bush? That is going to be one challenge for the grassroots.

Question: Can the grassroots bring the Democratic Party back?

Caddell: Well, that's exactly the point. And that's always what has happened. It is what happened with the Republican Party. It revitalized it from being the *me too* remainder party in Washington to the Republican candidates saying, "No, no, no. We're not for this anymore." And the question the Democratic Party has is whether we will challenge, because the money is there in the grassroots. As Elaine was saying, when you look at the polls of these people, they stand for something. Look at the contempt with which John Kerry raised the money he raised from those people. But he didn't want them to participate. He didn't want to give them an activist role. He didn't want their voice, he simply wanted their money.

And the question is whether, when the grassroots get fed up with that—being used by those kinds of people like the Kerry campaign—the Democratic Party will change.

Question: Should lower caps on political contributions be part of the Democrat message?

Caddell: Well, it should be, but guess who fought the caps? Guess who in this state fights that? I mean, I've never seen anything like it—anybody who wants to talk about the Democratic Party should look at the corruption of its leading state and what it has done—what it has done to Hispanics in this state, what it has done to the poor people in this state, who it serves in terms of being on the auction block and the fact that its public service unions are about to put this state under the ground by providing unholy pension deals that no ordinary person paying for it—taxpayers—will ever see in their lifetimes.

Question: Do you think Democrats should just write off religious voters?

Kamarck: No, I don't. Look. The Republicans worked really, really hard at religious voters, and the story of 2004 is not the story of evangelical voters, it is the story of Catholic voters—Roman Catholic voters. Where the Republicans made huge inroads was in Roman Catholics. Bush won them even though John Kerry is a Roman Catholic. Okay? So I think Democrats simply need to work the religious vote, and what I'm saying is that in going to religious voters, Democrats have a lot of things to talk about, okay? The new one on the horizon, by the way, is the environment, and the sense that environmentalism is part of what God intended us to do to be stewards of the earth. And the Democrats have a much stronger, you know, base on that, a much stronger history on that than the Republicans. And we don't have to win the entire religious vote. We just have to keep it from being so lopsided that in these close elections that we seem to be in, that's one of the things that gives it over. We're not going to win staunch right to lifers. Okay, we're not going to win people who are appalled at gay rights and stuff like that. That's a sort of silly thing for us to go after, but that doesn't mean that we shouldn't try to move in on a piece of that vote.

Caddell: First of all, one of the problems that's got to be gotten over here is something that we were talking about early about the elites—the big money elites in the Democratic Party—the secular, anti-religious people—and they are anti-religion. If anybody has a religion they look down with contempt. And they reflect that, and that is one of the problems here. For instance, Evangelicals from the South are very populist—I mean, Republicans get them on values issues, because the Democrats have abandoned their economic agenda. But there is a distinction between the leadership of that movement of Falwell or Robertson and the actual voters. They are very concerned about the environment, and one of the things that is happening in the South that no one is paying attention to, is for the first time the white Evangelicals are talking to blacks. That is a product of the fight over the gay marriage. You know, we aren't able to distinguish in my party between gay rights—the right to everyone in this country—and gay marriage. Well, the black Evangelicals for the first time have gotten together and started talking and forming alliances, and that will potentially do in [Democrats in] the South.

And do you know what issue they picked up on now? The environment and also about poor people. That is going to change politics. But you'll never know it in this party because the secular contempt—particularly in a place like Hollywood where I live—for people of religion and people of faith is so overwhelming that it sours people even to pay attention.

Beinart: If I could add just one thing on this. It seems to me the problem the Democratic Party has in trying to change talk about religion, and yet change the issues that people consider to be religious issues by putting poverty more at the forefront, is that these things really, it seems to me, are not going to be defined by politicians. They are going to be defined within your religious community.

The great advantage the Republicans have had, I think, is that there has basically been a decline of liberal mainline protestant churches, and within every religious community it's the most conservative branches that are growing, and so there you have people who actually have credibility, who people listen to, religious leaders who say, "No, no, don't listen to the Democrats, what we really think matter as religious questions are gay rights, abortion, etc., etc." And it seems to me a much bigger question—the Democrats have to find out where are the religious communities that you can tap into, where the people believe that the key religious issue is poverty and where the community is growing,, because otherwise, I think it's really not going to make a difference. If your particular minister is saying something about how Christianity should play itself out in the public sphere, what the Democratic Party is saying in Washington is not going to break through.

Caddell: Yeah, well, one thing would be to support the regulation of 527s, instead of standing up and defending them yesterday in the most appalling way that I've ever seen in my life. I mean, it was an embarrassment and made me almost physically ill to watch this. You don't need George Soros. George Soros did more damage to the Democratic Party in 2004 than he ever did to help it, I'll tell you that.

Kamarck: Let me add to that, that if George Soros had made the kinds of investments in his business career that he made in 2004, he would never have had all of this money that he has, okay?

Caddell: The difference was that in business he never would have listened to the people—the mediocrity of people that gathered around him to milk him for his money, to make those investments in the first place.

Kamarck: That's true, but I think you bring up a much bigger problem of the Democrats, which is a problem they need to confront on foreign policy, and I think going back to what Peter said, the fight that is going to happen within the Democratic Party, and it's starting to happen right now, is going to be over the use of force and whether or not America is a force for good or for ill in the world. That's going to be the fight, because there is a portion of the base—you hear it, you reflect it—that, you know, basically thinks that whenever America steps its foot into the world, it's up to no good.

The problem within the party is to somehow get to a point where we can be pro-American, we can believe in America's righteousness in the world, and convey that to the public, while also conveying that we think that this Iraq business was a complete disaster. I think this is really hard. I think it's the hardest intellectual problem that confronts the Democrats. I actually think that the other things, I mean, Ruy's concerns about the Democrats on the mechanics, I think actually those are working and moving in the right direction. I think there are a lot of things moving in the right direction. I think the foreign policy problems and those images, those senses that you get, are very deep and very difficult, and it could be the reason why Democrats fail in an election like 2008, unless they manage to somehow come to some solution to this problem.

Teixeira: Let me push on that a little bit. Again, it's hard to argue with the proposition that Democrats need to project a strong image on foreign policy and appear different than they have in the past. But what is that? This is what I'm having a hard time figuring out. What do you do about Iraq? And if what the Democrats want to say to people is we're for smart but tough, defense—that we're not afraid to use American power, though we want to use it in a smart way to provide global leadership and make the world a better place—what is the content of that? Specifically, what is the content of that relative to the Iraq occupation and war today, and what is the content of that for what appear to be the emerging global issues that we're probably going to face in the next few years? And what is the likely debate within the Democratic party going to be about that? I'm not so sure there are a lot of people in the Democratic Party that are reflexively and adamantly opposed to the use of U.S. power—for whom it doesn't matter where or why you use it, they would never support it. What is the evidence that such people have a large weight in the Democratic party?

Question: What is the evidence?

Beinart: There is some disturbing polling out there that I go into in my book, which comes out in June. Actually, what is interesting is the polling is much worse than in 2002. It's really the last year or so that you started to see much more than I think was there in the 1990s or in the first couple of years after 9-11—some of the kinds of things that Elaine has talked about, and it's because of anger over the Iraq War, and it may or may not be permanent. I would just say, I think that the answer for the Democratic Party on foreign party . . . sorry?

Teixeira: But what is the data?

Beinart: Well, for instance, if you look at the study that MIT did that is published in the *Boston Review*, which showed 59 percent of Democrats think Afghanistan was a good idea, 57 percent would use preemptive force to take out a terrorist camp. If you look at the thing that your own organization, The Center for American Progress poll did—they found that amongst Democrats if asked to rank their two top foreign policy priorities, destroying the Al Qaeda network came in tenth—sorry, self-described liberals, not Democrats. So there is some disturbing polling out there about Democrats on hard, national security questions.

The answer for Democrats, in some ways, is not that remote, because it's pretty much the answer that Bill Clinton and Tony Blair were getting to at the end of the 1990s, and it's very richly rooted in the Democratic Party's tradition, which is to say, in an era of globalization, America's security relies more and more on things that happen inside other countries—the diseases that they create, the environmental degradation they create, the potential financial instability intervention, and the potential for the creation of jihadist terrorists. But the United States does not have either the power or the legitimacy to go in and try to fix those countries itself, because if we do we will look like an empire, and in fact, we may become an empire. And so the answer is for much stronger empowered international institutions, the kind of international institution building that went on in the late 1940s, and needs to happen again so that we can actually—so that you can create institutions that can actually solve problems early, before you have things like bird flu, or another financial meltdown like what started in 1997, or another terrorist attack.

Teixeira: Well, Peter, I agree with all that, but do Democrats disagree with that? I mean, it sounds like a pretty easy sell.

Caddell: Well, I'm going to disagree with you on this one, because I'm going to tell you something. There is a huge part of the Democratic Party that acts like anything America does is evil and wrong. It's prevalent on college campuses everywhere in this country intellectually, and to pretend it's not there is wrong. The negative attitudes about the American military in some circles of the Democratic Party is there and real, and we might as well face up to it, and not pretend it isn't. And let me just finish. I want to tell you about foreign policy in the Democratic Party. Nobody paid attention. But during the campaign with John Kerry, he gave an interview about his foreign policy with the *Washington Post* and announced—it was unbelievable—that human rights will no longer be a lead priority in the Democratic Party. To show how we're really tough, we'll abandon human rights, and so forth, and he wasn't challenged on this, because that's the idea—pretending we're going to be strong—look at Darfur, for instance, as an issue.

You cannot be a party that stands against everything in the world, and also believes that your competition for hating George Bush is so great that you can't find things that transcends that. And there's much to criticize—there was before the war—but you know what, let me say something. I am tired of the criticism. These people getting up and saying, "Oh, George Bush got us in the war." Every Democrat who is not a member of the minority in Los Angeles and New York, voted for the war. The person who gave you the referendum was Mr. Berman. Howard Berman went and cut a deal behind Nancy Pelosi's back, to give George Bush a blank check on the war. So let's get this stuff out in front. The problem is we want to find out what we should do to look strong, as opposed to being strong. And an example of that is none other than Bill Clinton with Rwanda, for God's sake.

Kamarck: That's exactly where I was going to go, which is that during the White House years when I had a different portfolio, I kind of took for granted that oh, there were no military options on Rwanda. And I have since learned, by getting to know Samantha Powers and reading her book and hanging around people like Bob Rotberg, that in fact, there are many, many, many military options that the United States military is uniquely able to do, that in fact, with very little threat to American soldiers could, in fact, intervene quite successfully in situations like Rwanda, in situations like Darfur. So one way to perhaps start this conversation within the Democratic Party is to start with the things that these liberals like, like helping people in these horrible situations, and point out that, in fact, the only force on the face of the earth that can, in fact, effectively intervene is the United States military, and that if we don't as a party support the maintenance of a strong military, we will not be able to live up to our values on human rights in the world. And putting those two things together is, I think, the beginning of this conversation within the party.

Notes

1. See "The Politics of Polarization: A Third Way Report," (Washington, D.C., The Third Way) October, 2005.

2. See, William A. Galston and Elaine C. Kamarck, Ibid, for a summary of polling data on the recent history of voter perceptions of the Democratic Party in particular Chart #1, page 14.

3. James P. Womack, "Mr. Ford's Wrong Turn; Why Automakers Can't Blame Japan," *The Washington Post,* December 4, 2005, p. B01.

4. See, "Is Our Children Employable?" March, 24, 2006 at www.politicalcortex.com

5. Sholnn Freeman "Care Buyers losing faith in American automakers," *The Washington Post,* April 2, 2006.

6. For some background see, "A Qualitative Analysis of The Heritage Foundation and Pauly Group Proposals to Restructure the Health Insurance System," at www.cbo.gov/showdoc.cfm?index=4896&sequence=0. April 1994.

7. In 2005, 12.5percent of wage and salary workers were union members, down from 20.3 percent in 1983 and over 30 percent in the 1950s. Furthermore, of union members today the majority are public sector employees. News release, United States Department of Labor, Bureau of Labor Statistics, January 20, 2006. http://www.bls.gov/cps.

8. Most conservatives are as appalled at the spend and spend record of the Bush Administration as are Democrats. See, for instance, "$20,000 per household, The Highest Level of Federal Spending Since World War II," by Brian M. Riedl, Backgrounder #1710, The Heritage Foundation, Washington, D.C.

9. Quoted in *The Washington Post,* January 31, 2006, CQ Transcript.

10. See Stephen Slivinski, "Bush Beats Johnson: Comparing the Presidents," (Washington, D.C., The Cato Institute) Tax and Budget Bulletin, # 26, October 2005. "Contrast that with Bush's presidency so far. He has presided over massive increases in almost every category. This is a dramatic change from previous presidents, when increases in defense spending were offset by cuts in non-defense spending…"

11. See Galston and Kamarck, Ibid, page 16 for a listing of positions on defense and foreign policy going back to the 1976 election.

12. Ibid, page 29.

13. See, *Campaign for President: The Managers Look at 2004,"* edited by The Institute of Politics, John F. Kennedy School of Government, Harvard University, (Lanham, Maryland, Rowman and Littlefield Publishers) 2005.

14. See Samantha Powers, *A Problem from Hell: America and the Age of Genocide,*

15. See National Election Poll Data, 2000.

16. Ibid.

17. Galston and Kamarck, Ibid, page 42.

18. Ibid, page 43.

19. Brendan Miniter, "What Would Jesus Drive?" *The Wall Street Journal,* November 25, 2002.

20. See *Small Donors and Online Giving: A Study of Donors to the 2004 Presidential Campaign,* Institute for Politics, Democracy and the Internet, at www.ipdi.org, (Washington, D.C., George Washington University) March 2006.

21. Ibid, page 4.

22. Ibid, page 24.

Bibliography

"A Qualitative Analysis of The Heritage Foundation and Pauly Group Proposals to Restructure the Health Insurance System." www.cbo.gov/showdoc.cfm?index=4896&sequence=0. April 1994.

Campaign for President: The Managers Look at 2004. Edited by The Institute of Politics, John F. Kennedy School of Government, Harvard University. Lanham, MD: Rowman and Littlefield Publishers, 2005.

"Is Our Children Employable?" March, 24, 2006 at www.politicalcortex.com

"News Release." United States Department of Labor, Bureau of Labor Statistics, January 20, 2006. http://www.bls.gov/cps.

Small Donors and Online Giving: A Study of Donors to the 2004 Presidential Campaign. Institute for Politics, Democracy and the Internet, at www.ipdi.org. Washington, D.C., George Washington University, March 2006.

Freeman, Sholnn. "Car Buyers losing faith in American automakers." *The Washington Post,* April 2, 2006.

Galston, William and Elaine Kamarck. "The Politics of Polarization: A Third Way Report." Washington, D.C., The Third Way, October, 2005.

Miniter, Brendan. "What Would Jesus Drive?" *The Wall Street Journal,* November 25, 2002.

Powers, Samantha. *A Problem from Hell: America and the Age of Genocide.* New York: Harper, 2003.

Riedl, Brian M. "$20,000 per Household, The Highest Level of Federal Spending Since World War II." Backgrounder #1710. The Heritage Foundation, Washington, D.C.

Slivinski, Stephen. "Bush Beats Johnson: Comparing the Presidents," Tax and Budget Bulletin, # 26, October 2005. Washington, D.C., The Cato Institute, October 2005.

Womack, James P. "Mr. Ford's Wrong Turn; Why Automakers Can't Blame Japan." *The Washington Post,* December 4, 2005, B01.

Chapter Two

A New Direction for the Parties?

Hon. Timothy Roemer

It's great for me to be at this beautiful campus and part of this very interesting program. We got off to a great start this morning, as Democrats do. We have spirited debates, and we don't hold anything back. So you invited just a terrific panel to start things off, and you have a terrific Republican panel coming up this afternoon. I run into many people on that panel around Washington out in the field and occasionally on Fox News. So you will be also informed and entertained by them.

I am delighted to be back in California. I started my undergraduate work down at University of California San Diego, and in spite of the great weather and the beaches and the volley ball, I finished at the University of California at San Diego, where I just recently saw many of my friends who I graduated with in 1979, and they are still at the University of California at San Diego, enjoying life down there.

Much has changed for me since I graduated. My wife Sally and I have four children and they range in age from five (Grace), to thirteen (Patrick). We have two boys and two girls. I was snuggling in bed with my five-year-old the other day and as only a five-year-old can do, she said to me, "Daddy, how was your day?" I said, "Grace, where did you come up with that question?" She said, "Daddy, I hear Mommy ask that to you all the time. How was your day?" And we're getting ready to read a story and turn the light out, and say our prayers, and she looks at me and says, "Daddy, answer the question."

I said, "Okay, Grace, I had a great day. Two great things happened to me. This morning you were in our bed and woke me up and that was a wonderful way to start the day, and tonight your sister had a birthday party and I've never seen her happier celebrating her birthday. Great, great day."

Two seconds of silence, and she said, "So, Daddy, what was better, Sarah or me?" And I said, "Grace, you can't ask me a question like that. That would be like me saying to you, 'Who do you love more, Mommy or Daddy,'" and she said, "Daddy that's easy, I love Mommy a lot more than you."

You ask a tough question and you get a tough answer. Kids make choices and adults make choices. We choose where we're going to eat our lunch. I'm grateful so many of you showed up to listen to what I have to say about political parties. We all make choices about what political party we belong to. I happened to have picked the Democratic Party many years ago for three reasons:

1. Because of my family, my mother and father, diehard Democrats taught us that the party was the best way to go in the future, and you wouldn't have a choice growing up.
2. It was with my Catholicism, my faith, that politics was a venue to help other people.
3. It was RFK. When the sister in my fifth grade class said, "Who's going to coordinate Bobby Kennedy's campaign to try to get him to win in the thirty votes?" my hand shot up and I was off to the races in politics, later running for office myself.

Those were some of my thought processes, feelings, and emotions in selecting a political party. Some of you have different reasons for doing it. Today as so many of us Democrats sat on that panel, we are in a time of poison, of gridlock, of grassroots change, of frustration. Will the political parties have some kind of contribution to make to funnel that support toward new policies to help us solve problems today? Or will the parties be less relevant? Will the Internet be more relevant? Will money take on more importance? Will a third-party candidate emerge as one did in Israel? We don't have the answers to some of these questions. I think Elaine Kamarck said you have to look back into history to try to move forward.

I'm going to try to comment on three different areas to give you my views as to where we might go on the Democratic side, what ideas might come forward, what might benefit us in terms of party organization.

First of all, I'm going to talk a little bit about some of the organizational rules. What might the party do to become more effective? Especially concerning the sense of frustration out there on the part of our electorate. For example, Indiana, my home state, a state that President Bush won sixty-one to thirty-nine, has probably two and a half House races in play to date, two and a half in one of the most conservative states in the country. Why is that and what can we do about it? I'm going to talk about five organizational principals that I think would probably help the Democratic Party win in those kinds of instances.

Two, I want to talk a little bit about the neo-conservative critique—because every time I ran for office in Northern Indiana, and was blessed with winning all six times—my rule was every time you got up when you ran against an incumbent, you said three things why that person should be fired and three things why you should be hired. What is it that I bring to this job that would make you want to take your time to go to the polls on election day and cast that ballot for a new idea, a different kind of candidate, somebody that hopefully will go to Washington and implement the kind of changes and values and the forums that the people in that district would want.

And lastly, I want to talk a little bit about (and I won't spend as much time on this because it was covered so well, I believe, by the panel this morning) a narrative for the Democratic Party—not so much a contract for America, but maybe a story about where the Democrats need to go on three key issues.

So first of all, organizational rules: The first one I'll call the "perfect list." Doris Kearns Goodwin has written a masterful biography on Abraham Lincoln, this political genius who not only gave some of the greatest speeches in the history of the world, but who loved to tell a story to make you laugh. The human side of Lincoln comes out so brilliantly in this book. But also what came out is his keen political nature and his ability to work the grassroots. On Page 89, Abe Lincoln talks about how to organize his local precinct in 1840, something our Democratic party could probably learn a bit from today. The quote is the following:

> "Precinct lists were divided by each precinct captain into sections of ten who reside most convenient to each other." Kearns goes on to write, "The captain of each section was responsible to each person face to face and would procure his pledge and vote as early in the day as possible.

> "And then in the 1840 presidential election of William Henry Harrison, Lincoln and Joshua Speed took it a step further and they wanted to develop a circular that was designed to keep a constant eye on those doubtful voters. How was this person going to end up going to the polls? Who were they going to vote for—the Whig candidate, the Democratic candidate, who will they vote for? And they were to submit monthly reports to the central committee about their progress speaking to those ten or twenty or thirty key voters."

I think one of the things that we saw in the last election, and Michael Malbin talked a little bit about this and the influence of money—a fascinating presentation—is that Democrats did some things better than Republicans and Republicans maybe used the Internet to communicate, and Democrats (with Howard Dean) raised more small contributions and little money, but Democrats did not do a good job in the last election of knocking on that door with somebody who lived in that neighborhood, who knew what church they went to or what Synagogue, or if they didn't go to church and they went to the baseball field on a Sunday morning.

The Republicans were very good at sending somebody locally from that neighborhood into that neighborhood. The Democrats thought they were good about getting some people from New York City to volunteer their time and go to West Virginia and knock on those doors and say, "Who are you voting for?" But in Ohio those Republicans were saying, "Hey, Joe, how is your son doing on the baseball team? I saw him play the other day. I hope all is going well. Do you need a ride to the store or to pick up anything there? By the way, what's the big issue for you coming up? Who are you thinking about voting for?" Democrats have to help develop the perfect list.

Secondly, the iPod. I was putting my eleven-year-old to bed the other day. This is the theme in the Roemer family with four kids. We're always putting people to bed, and my eleven-year-old had his iPod on. I thought he was listening to U2, and I said, "Hey, you know the rules, Matthew, get it off and get a book in your hands. We read for a half an hour every night." He said, "Dad, I am reading." I said, "No you're not. Don't try to pull that one on me—I'm getting old, but I'm not that old. Get that iPod off." He said, "No, Dad, I'm reading." I said, "Okay, give me the iPod and get a book." He handed it to me and said, "Dad, just plug it in your ear." I listened to it, "Chapter 4, Tom Sawyer." He was reading.

How do we develop this technology when we go get that perfect list to go to that door in North Dakota, Southern Indiana, Pennsylvania, Ohio, and we play a device that shows that voter what we're going to do to help them on access to healthcare?

The Democratic Party has their answer right there, if we can develop it, on national security. How do we do this? The technology is very close. It's there in many ways. How do we develop it and communicate on the ground down in the grassroots with the voters?

Thirdly, scheduling Ross Perot. Who'd want that job—anybody? When I ran for Congress throughout the 1990s as a Democrat and beat a Republican incumbent for the job, we picked up very quickly on the fact that Ross Perot got a certain segment of the independent vote in '92 and '96, but even before '96, we started scheduling many of my activities into areas where we could pick up that independent vote. If Ross Perot got 28 percent of the vote in a particular precinct, I went door-to-door in that precinct. If Ross Perot got 20 percent of the vote in a particular area we would hold a town meeting—pancake breakfast— and make sure we hit the parade in that area. And we wouldn't just walk down the center of the parade, we would get off the parade route and talk to people and listen to them, and figure out what their concerns were—what their needs were. So Ross Perot would be somebody that we would look to, to schedule our events, to pay attention, as Pat Caddell said, to what people really think, and tell them when you disagree with them. Let them know. "Well, I don't agree with you on that particular issue, but maybe the next one we will agree on."

Thirdly, old values, new ideas. We need to be a party, a Democratic Party that takes on new issues. Elaine said left or right—sometimes it's not left or right, it's new, what's in your soul and what's in your gut.

For me, I think both the Democratic Party and the Republican Party are wrong and need to develop a new idea on abortion. We have 10 percent of the Democrats and 10 percent of the Republicans defining the issue and raising the money for the rest of the constituency in America. They gridlocked the issue. Do we still have 1.3 million abortions a year, like we had ten years ago, today? Yes, even though the Republicans have had the House of Representatives for ten years and the White House for five. There's still the same number of abortions.

So let's get a new idea. Let's break out of this gridlock. Let's have you folks determine what goes on, to cut down on the number of abortions every year. And we've got an idea to do it—an old value and a new idea. And I think the Democratic Party can win with a new policy that doesn't try to overturn a law or go to the Supreme Court. It lays out innovatively, dynamically, ideas that Republicans can't talk about: Contraception—let's prevent the unwanted pregnancy in the first place, and even though my church does not agree with that, I disagree with them.

Then, let's put our money where our mouth is. Let's put some money into pre-natal healthcare. Let's put our money and our work under the tax code for adoption tax credits that are permanent and help defray some of the costs of that life coming into the world. Let's work together on a women, infant and children program that funds the poorer women who are inordinately part of the higher percentage that pick the abortion because there is no support system for them to go to.

When I was in the DNC (Democratic National Committee) race I can't tell you the number of even our base voters—African American and Hispanic voters who would come up to me, very quietly sometimes. They didn't vote (I don't think) for me, but they said, "You are right on this issue. Abortion is a tragedy."

Fourth, I would say this is in the great tradition of our party. Democrats work on ideas to try to cut down on the number of people that are hungry. They try to cut down on the number of people that are homeless. They try to eliminate the number of people dying of AIDS. Why can't we be the party that reduces the number of abortions from 1.3 to 1 million, to 500,000, to 400,000 with that two-prong innovative, dynamic approach? Sixty to 70 percent of the country, I think, would support it. An old value—human life—a new idea trying to break the gridlock of Washington special interests. I think most people want us to do something about that issue.

And fifth—the fifth organizing principle (I've got five more, but I won't go into them today) is it's not only what you say; it's where you say it. When I was in Congress, I oftentimes didn't want to do this, but I knew it was the right thing to do, my staff would say, "You know, you're going to the Chamber of Commerce today." Oh, man, they'd grill me. Man, they asked me some tough questions. "And then you're going to the Lions Club and then you're going to the Farmers. And then you're going to go talk to the mega church out in Granger."

And it wasn't so much that we have to change our soul and our heart as a Democratic Party—we don't have to wear religion on our sleeves, because it comes naturally to us to talk about helping the poor. We want to do something about the number of poor in the United States. And we should want to do something, as Peter brought out, about the number of the poor in the world, because they could be part of this global economy.

We talk about global warming and I think more and more people know that that is a problem. I worked recently with Reverend Richard Sizik with the evangelicals on Darfur and on the environment. If Democrats can simply say what they believe in on balanced budgets and how we worked to get there in '97—we made tough choices on spending. The budget, the environment, helping the poor, a new idea on abortion—I think we're going to do surprisingly well talking to those audiences, and maybe instead of losing them 80/20, Democrats lose them 70/30.

But you know what, Pat Caddell, that's a lot of wins across the country when you can start getting into that kind of changing of the outcome of those voter groups. Don't change what you say. Keep your soul and your heart and your emotion. But just go say it to different audiences. Don't keep saying, "I've got to go talk to the MoveOn.org people and increase my base." In these two and a half seats in Indiana that are in play, you're not going to increase your base with the moveon.org. They're there—they're not growing. With the Chamber and the other groups and churches, synagogues, and the mosques, those are growing populations.

My second major point, the neoconservative critiques: I don't know how many of you saw Newt Gingrich on the air the other day and he said something about "had enough" as a policy that the Democrats could use. I actually did some research on this and it wasn't Newt Gingrich. It was a guy named Carl, not Karl Rove—A guy by the name of Carl Frost in 1946. He came up with the idea of "Had enough?" as a Republican, because the Democrats had been in control he thought long enough, and they hadn't solved some of the basic economic problems, so he came up with "Had enough? Vote Republican."

Well, imagine if the Democrats can begin to say that four and a half years after 9-11, we don't even have a national strategy to invest in protecting the nuclear power plants (104 of them), yet we are building and buying bridges to nowhere, "Had enough?"

Or we could talk about Katrina. Blowing the veil off the scab of poverty in our country where this city will never be the same. One in ten businesses returned, poor people scattered throughout Texas and Arkansas and we can't even communicate with our local first responders four years after 9-11. We have people in helicopters trying to talk to people in boats to rescue our own citizens on the roof of a major city, and we can't do it. Bangladesh, as you might remember, one of the poorest countries of the world, offered the United States of America foreign assistance of $50,000. "Have you had enough?"

The Dubai World Ports deal, our critical infrastructure to protect our ports—not a port in Maine, New York, New Jersey, Miami, Philadelphia, New Orleans—the President wants to put that critical infrastructure under the control of Middle Eastern countries. I don't care what religion they are, I don't care what region of the world it is, but the record of that country was blemished and spotted as noted by the 9-11 Commission, and we should not put our critical infrastructure and our port security under the charge of that particular country. "Had enough?"

Debt—the President has talked about fiscal responsibility and vetoing a bill on port security, but he hasn't vetoed a single bill that is spending too much of our tax payers' money. "Had enough?"

You get the message. And if you get "Had Enough" on buttons, Internet, bumper stickers, it's a much more compelling message for the Democratic Party, than simply pulling up behind a car that has a W scratched out bumper sticker. You're not going to follow that bumper sticker very long if it's only you want to get rid of George W. Bush and he's not even on the ballot. What are we about as a party?

So what are we about as a party? You saw how difficult it is for Democrats to talk about where we go next. And I will just briefly because I've probably taken a lot of time and I know you probably have some tough questions for me, let me tell it in a narrative the three issues that I think are the most important and that I believe Democrats can rally behind. I think that probably what Pat Caddell said, the grassroots, the anger, the disenfranchisement of people out there are growing and building, and to say that we need almost a new American Revolution today may not be quite overstating it.

First and foremost, I think Democrats should talk about national security, not because Karl Rove thinks it's the most important issue for Republicans to talk about in the 2006 election, that's what he said in his speech to Republicans about a month and a half ago. I think that is the compelling issue for Democrats to talk about today, not to be defensive, not to try to insulate ourselves from something, but because that is the most important issue to every single American today in one way or another. When you add up Iraq, the war on terrorism, Jihadism, it usually ends up that 33 to 38 percent of the people are most concerned about this issue.

Now Republicans like to talk about strong national security policy and Ruy Teixiera talked about this debate between some in the party and some not in the party about the doves that don't want to use the military even to go out and get somebody like Osama Bin Laden. Or do they want to use it to help in Darfur? Maybe not.

The Democrats need to be able to articulate beyond tough and smart. Maybe our symbol is the owl—not the hawk or the dove—but the owl that has the talons that can fight for what we believe in, projecting our principles out into the world for good to try to bring more people into the global economic system, our free enterprise system—the system that came up with every single technological innovation over the twentieth century—a system that helped spread more economic opportunities and prosperity and freedom to more people, and more peace.

We should be able to talk about an owl-type of Democratic policy. That it is not only the military that we should be able to use effectively, and transform that military from building up F-22s at $200 million a pop—fighters that were designed to evade the Soviet radar and try to make sure that we are building our special operations forces and that we are trying to build the next generation of carbon fiber laser guided bombs, not 2,500 pound bombs that might have been dropped on the Soviet Union.

How do we make sure your tax payer money is spent wisely on defense and homeland security? How do we get a smarter policy, a more confident government out of that expenditure? I think every American wants to hear about that. I think every American knows that when we're fighting this war on Jihadism, it could be a twenty, a thirty—Newt Gingrich said a seventy-year struggle.

And it's not checkers. It's not the good guy versus the bad guy. It's not you move once, I'll move once. It's three-dimensional chess, where we need a transformed military that can effectively strike, we need homeland security that actually invests in the long term and doesn't pork-barrel spend.

And we need to win the hearts and minds. We need economic and educational opportunities so that that a prospective jihadist doesn't sign up for that conveyer belt that ends with bombs strapped on their chests to try to blow up Americans in New York, Spaniards in Madrid, and British in Great Britain.

We need to convince them that we have the best economic system. The best system of freedom in the world. That's the hearts and minds and that's what

Don Rumsfeld said the other day. When asked are we winning this war, Secretary Rumsfeld said "I give our government about a D." That's our own Secretary of Defense grading his own government.

We have to do better to win this long-term war with the hearts and minds by using our soft power. And as I said about Reverend Richard Sizik, more and more of the religious community want us to talk, not because it's the right politics, we want to talk about what we do about the number of people living in the world on less than a dollar a day. And if we can gradually bring them into the economic system of the United States of America, the free enterprise system, not only is that the right thing to do and the golden rule, that's the right thing to do for jobs here, exporting to other countries and making them members of the world community.

Secondly, I would say very briefly, that in addition to national security, we've heard a lot of Democrats talk about the rich and the poor. I would say let us revive the American dream. Whether you're making $30,000 or $100,000, whether you're black or brown, whether you're gay, how do we get more people to feel like there are not obstacles in front of them every step of the way, whether there be an unfair tax system, whether it's corporate cronyism, or corporate welfare that we talked about this morning, how do we change this system so that this dream is again alive for most of the American people? There are too many obstacles and there are too many barnacles on the engine of our free enterprise system. We need to clean it up. We need to change it.

The third issue I would have Democrats talk about is renewing, repairing, and reforming our democracy. How do we make sure when so many people are not confident that we're even counting the votes right that we are listening to the voices of this country. More and more people don't believe that they are part of this great system.

The founder of our great Democratic party, Thomas Jefferson said we are the last best hope of the world. Yet when the Carter Center brought observers from China to our country in 2000, and they brought them here to show them our great system, sadly, it was bad timing (we're talking about the presidential election in 2000). The Chinese asked a series of questions: "How is it that you don't have the votes counted in one of the biggest states? How is it that you have one-party dominance? How is it that you folks here in America have so much money in your system in special interests, and you want us to emulate your system and take it back to China? With all of these problems, this is the great system?"

We must bring this revival and hope back to our great republic. We must give people the confidence and the opportunity that if they want to run for public office some day they don't have to be a millionaire. If they have a good idea for legislation they don't have to have a lobbyist. If they have a brilliant idea to help somebody else get elected, they can participate in this system again whether they are Democratic or Republican. That is what this great system is all about—opportunity. It's going away, but we can bring it back. This great country with participation can bring it back.

Let me just conclude by saying you've been very patient—I'm trying to use up all my time so you don't have any tough questions that I have to answer.

Now Peter Beinart warned me about doing this, but I'll do it anyway. Isaiah Chapter 58: Repairers of the breach. We are all called to be repairers of the breach. We have worked hard with fierce determination to try to repair the breach in Louisiana and New Orleans, but there is an even bigger breach of confidence in this country in our government in making it work, in making it accountable, in restoring the American dream.

Let's repair that breach together. That will truly bring this country forward, united rather than divided, rich again in the principles that our founding fathers put forward.

Thank you so much for your time and your opportunity, and I'll be happy to try to answer questions.

Questions and Answers

Question: Thank you very much for your time. I heard a reoccurring theme with restoring the American dream. It's good to see that you represent the Democratic Party and our elected officials in D.C. do have—even in the back of your mind— the ideology that the American dream is still possible, and the hope that we can get there. But it also reminds me of what's happening in France right now with the young people who are protesting the labor laws that they are trying to inflict. But also here in the United States where the last thirty years trade unionism dropped off and decreased. We saw last summer the AFL-CIO (American Federation of Labor–Congress of Industrial Organizations) has taken a large split where there were about seven major labor unions that split away from the AFL-CIO because of the fact that their organizing efforts have diminished by so much, but their mantra is to restore the American dream. So it's ironic that you hear this reoccurring theme.

Based on history and what we see in the world when it comes to people organizing unions, do you see the trade union movement in this country being a catalyst in helping to restore the American dream, and where do you see American policy on the Democrat or Republican side playing into that, and really helping people to see the American dream without isolating people who may not necessarily from an ideological standpoint agree with you.

Timothy Roemer: See, that's why I didn't want to get to Q and A.

Very good, very tough question, and I'll try my best to give a spot on answer here. First of all, I would slightly disagree with Elaine a little bit from this morning, although I think we're probably going to see a stabilization in the number of the labor community. I don't think it's going to go away soon, but I'm speaking from the Midwest. Where I come from, an area where there are a lot of union workers—carpenters, pipe fitters, UAW (United Auto Workers union) workers, who are also going through troubles—you talk about this American dream that's evaporating for some and that we need to revive for our country.

We just had an announcement in the Midwest that 30,000 General Motors jobs are going to be gone forever, 30,000 Ford jobs are going to be gone forever, and for us in the Midwest, we know that there are six jobs associated with every one of those auto jobs. And those are manufacturing jobs with pensions and with decent healthcare, so we're looking not at 60,000 jobs leaving the United States of America, we're looking at somewhere around 200,000 or 300,000.

How do we get those back? What do we do to try to make sure that when somebody loses that job and they're fifty-five years old, that there's just not some training program that's talked about as part of a NAFTA (North American Free Trade Agreement) vote, that may or may not ever appear.

There is a program in the United States throughout the country that takes workers that might have been in that steel mill, that trains them for a job in an Intel plant creating the chip of the future, and that chip producing plant isn't built in Ireland.

They just had a Texas Instruments plant built outside Dallas, I think, in Richardson, and they went to the community—they went to the labor community, they went to the business community, the engineering community—and they said, "We can't be competitive here in the United States unless we build this building for $180,000 less than you have proposed. We need different elbow joints and the pipes for the water, for heating, and it will save us money." They listed five or six different things they could do working together as a community to build that plant, and they would build it there because it was close to a research plant and there would be American jobs. That's the model that revives the American dream.

How do we put those kind of cooperative ventures together so that we maintain jobs, decent pensions, good healthcare, and we can compete in the world? I think that's one of the new models. I don't think it's just looking at building labor back to where it was or letting labor go away. I think those are the kinds of new paradigms hopefully that can get us answers on this problem of how to create jobs that manufacture the kind of scrubber that will go on a plant in China and we won't have the hole in the atmosphere over Toledo, Ohio that directly affects Americans. It's a global problem, it's an American problem.

Question: Are you arguing that every Democrat should run on your principles?

Roemer: Having experience with this when I ran the first time (in 1990), I ran against an incumbent. It was a conservative district. Some Democrats said, "Agh! Don't run. You can't win in that seat." Some Democrats said, "We have a forty-seat advantage, we don't need another Democrat." Other people sent me policy position papers from the DCCC (Democratic Congressional Campaign Committee) that might have worked in New York City. They wouldn't have worked in South Bend, Indiana. They weren't what I believed, anyway.

I think you have to be your own candidate. You can't run cookie cutter approaches. You can't tell people what to believe in. Our national security issues, reviving the American dream and the economy and values or as I stated in the third principle, is the value of democracy important? Yes! But do I think every

Democrat has to run on that to be successful? Absolutely not. No! We shouldn't make them.

I was in Southern Indiana with a Democratic candidate a month ago. He is a sheriff—Brad Ellsworth. He's running against a Republican incumbent and we got done with the homeland security forum. The first question from the press was, "What are you going to do about Iraq if you become Congressman, Mr. Ellsworth?" And the first words out of his mouth, you could tell, were heartfelt. "You know what, I hope our troops do the right thing there. I hope we succeed." And then he went on to talk about how badly we need to change what has taken place over the last three years, and how many mistakes have been made, but here are the three things that we need to do to change things in Iraq.

Now, I couldn't have scripted that for him. That was what he believed, and I think that's what our candidates have to be able to do. National security—do they have to learn that national security might be the most important question? Yes. But I don't think the Democratic Party should be able to say to every single Democrat from Southern Indiana to Oregon to Southern Florida, "Here's what you've got to say about our people dying in Iraq." I might have a very different view than a Democrat in another part of the country on our troops and how we succeed in a critically important area of the world.

Question: Hi, I'm Julie. I'm a student here as well. My question is, you just explained how each candidate needs its own individual message, and each congressional district is so different, but in the 2008 presidential election, what kind of candidate will it take to unify, and particularly, who, if you have a preference? And, also, what issue. . . .

Roemer: Oh, no, you won't get me to go there!

Question: Or what issue do you think could unify the Democratic Party?

Roemer: I don't think the Democratic Party needs particularly to be unified right now. I think we need to have some good old fights, some drag 'em out debates, some real heart-to-heart about what direction we go as a party. Now I sensed frustration from every one of those Democratic panelists this morning that we are not in touch enough with the people around this country on a lot of these issues.

You go into Southern Indiana, a very conservative part of the country, there is some populism all over the country that the Dubai Port scandal brought up. It wasn't just a critical infrastructure issue—are we safer in the post–9-11 world? It was, for instance, in Indiana, the Governor is talking about selling off our toll roads to a Spanish-Australian company.

It's about jobs going to Mexico under NAFTA. It's about what my kids are going to do if we keep losing legal jobs and tax accounting jobs, let alone blue collar jobs. The white collar jobs are going. So how do we come up with a national security, global strategy that Democrats can embrace that helps the poor and brings more people into the global economy, and that tries to make sure we make tough fiscal decisions on our own balanced budget and spending issues—that modernizes our defense system, that produces manufacturing capability that other countries are going to buy and do something about our trade deficit.

I think we've got to have these battles because we're not going to be unified in '08 if we don't have these battles in '06. So I think that's a very import exercise for us to go through, and it's not just to exercise and flex our muscles, and "Oh, I've got to hear Roemer talk about national security or education or abortion again. Man! I'm so sick of him." It's about how are we going to develop the best kind of policies to go forward and represent people to solve some of these very significant problems in our country in the next few years.

Who do I think are the best candidates? I don't know who the best candidates are yet. I think we've got a lot of good candidates who would make excellent presidents. I also think that these candidates that are running for president and senators and other offices should raise that money for great '06 candidates, rather than sucking up money for their own aspirations in '08. We've got six or seven people running for President. That's a lot of money being sucked out of the system, and if we can get into a situation where the Democrats don't have thirty-five seats in play but they have forty-five or fifty-five seats in play, that money is going to be critically important and right now it's going off to different states and not able to be helpful—and it's a race that's still got to be determined.

Question: Would you consider running for office again?

Roemer: Oh, no, not me. My wife said, "Get out of Congress so you can see your four kids." I'm having a good time in the private sector. I love this because I've heard all of my life from the Chamber of Commerce that Democrats don't know how to balance the budget, they don't know how to run a business, they don't know how to be accountable. I'm in the private sector and I'm loving it. I'm making more money than I was before and I'm getting out there doing all kinds of things.

Question: Are you a member of the Democratic National Committee ?

Roemer: Am I a member of the DNC? No, sir, I'm not. No. Maybe that was one of the reasons that when I ran I was advised by some of my supporters in Congress that I wasn't a member of DNC and therefore I would be at a disadvantage. Quite frankly, when we got into that race I thought we probably had about an 18 percent or 20 percent chance of winning that race. Governor Dean had just run for President. He knew all 448 voters very, very well. He had a lot of their support. Our DNC voters, like the RNC (Republican National Committee) voters, are kind of outside of even the party framework. They are much more liberal in the DNC than even our liberal wing is, and I didn't have a very good chance as a moderate Democrat. But I thought it was important to get some messages out and some new ideas out there, and although it was a very difficult race for me at times, walking into audiences that weren't very happy with me, I think it was good experience for me to go through, and hopefully for our party.

Question: How do you think Howard Dean is doing as DNC Chairman?

Roemer: Well, you know, I ran against Howard Dean, so I'm probably not the best or most objective person to ask this question. But I would say that Governor Dean is probably doing some good things in party building. I heard him say many, many times that party building was critically important, whether it's Indiana, North Dakota, or Kansas, we need to have a fifty-state strategy, and he's absolutely right on that. You can't roll the dice with eighteen states and you lose one of them and you don't win. We can't be a national party. I don't think we've won a southern electoral vote in the last two Presidential elections. How can you be a national party? How can you not compete for southern votes? My wife gets really adamant about that because she's from Louisiana and her father served in the United States Senate as a Democrat, you know, four or five different elections as a southern Democrat.

We can win in those seats. If you're going to talk, talk about what we believe in. It doesn't mean that a southern Democrat from Alabama has to agree completely with a northern New Englander from Maine, but we've got to be more competitive, and I think Governor Dean is trying to invest in that party building with executive directors, hopefully, more specifically, some of the things that I outlined on technology and grassroots building and perfect precinct lists, and getting the active people involved from the neighborhood, rather than shipping people in the last two months of an election. But he's got his work cut out for him. I think he's doing a good job, and my hat's off to him.

Chapter Three

The Republicans' Strategy for the Future

Andrew E. Busch

Roundtable: Michael Barone, Andrew E. Busch,
Hugh Hewitt, and William Kristol

On the surface, the Republican Party is in a better place than it has been at any time since the 1920s. It has controlled both houses of Congress for more than decade, with a brief interlude caused by Senator James Jeffords' defection in mid-2001. It has now controlled the White House, as well, for the last five years. Even at the state level, Republicans have held a majority of governorships without interruption since the 1994 elections. Not since the 1920s have Republicans held the presidency and both houses of Congress at the same time for more than two years. It is clear that Republicans have come a long way since 1968 or 1980 and that it is reasonable to consider it the governing party in America, at least for the moment.

There are four key reasons that Republicans have gone from a seemingly hopeless minority to control of the elected branches of the federal government in the last four decades. First, starting with Barry Goldwater's small donor appeals and Ray Bliss's organizational renovation as chairman of the Republican National Committee, Republicans have attained tactical superiority in a number of fields. Most recently, in 2002 and 2004, they succeeded in marrying new technology to old-fashioned grassroots mobilization to form a turnout machine that beat the Democrats at what used to be indisputably their game.

Second, Republicans have benefited significantly from the development of a conservative ideological infrastructure consisting of think tanks, journals, and foundations capable of challenging liberal dominance in the intellectual world and advancing conservative ideas and policy prescriptions. This infrastructure ranges from the Heritage Foundation to the *Weekly Standard*.

Third, the strengthened GOP position has been owed in part to a dramatic change in the shape of the media since the 1960s. The "new media," consisting of talk radio, cable television, and internet blogging, has been more conservative and Republican-leaning than not. The decentralized, mostly-conservative new media has increasingly served as a check on the predominantly liberal "old media," providing voters with an alternative source for news and analysis.

These first three causes for the Republican surge, however, have been largely technical and instrumental. Most important to the rolling Republican realignment of the last forty years has been the confluence of ideas, events, and demography. In particular, Barry Goldwater and Ronald Reagan articulated a set of political principles and policy positions the validity of which seemed to many previously skeptical Americans to have been largely verified by experience. Goldwater's (and, in general, conservatism's) critique of Great Society liberalism rang increasingly true as the 1960s and 1970s wore on, while Americans also noticed the coincidence of Reagan's (and, in general, conservatism's) call for limited government and the revival of the nation's fortunes in the 1980s. Republicans made a sustained argument, and could plausibly claim to be vindicated by events, both good (when they were in power) and bad (when they were not). Meanwhile, Democrats inadvertently invited voters to associate them with a weak foreign policy, an overbearing domestic government, and radical social views in ways ranging from the nominations of George McGovern and Walter Mondale to the Clinton health reform proposal to endorsement of a number of liberal judicial decisions on social matters.

Demographically, Republicans gained a more sympathetic audience for their argument from the declining proportion of Americans affiliated with organized labor and the rising proportion of Americans owning stock. They also gained from massive population shifts from the rustbelt to the sunbelt, which added congressional seats and electoral votes to more conservative regions of the country. In all, Republicans succeeded in putting together a coalition much like the coalition touted in the *National Review*'s long project of "fusionism," a sunbelt coalition consisting of economic conservatives or libertarians, cultural traditionalists, and foreign policy hawks.

So why are Republicans feeling so sour in 2006? Republicans, now having held power in Congress for over a decade, have become stagnant and tainted by corruption. There is a sense that the revolutionaries of 1994 have now become what they once opposed, a problem starkly symbolized by Duke Cunningham's boat house and Ted Stevens' appropriations earmarks for bridges to nowhere. As well, the Republican coalition, considerably bigger than it was in 1975, is now that much harder to hold together. Both of these problems are connected to the Republicans' rise to (slender) majority status; and it is not clear that they can be entirely avoided as long as that status remains intact, though they might be mitigated.

The third reason for Republican discontent is a growing sense of philosophical malaise—a sense that the party has become unmoored from some of its most basic philosophical commitments, that elected Republicans have stopped seeking power for the sake of important principles and are now engaged in seeking power for its own sake. Democrats face a version of this problem themselves, with criticism spearheaded by MoveOn.org and likeminded liberal activists who echo Howard Dean's 2004 call for restoration of the "Democratic wing of the Democratic party." However, for Republicans, a party that has long styled itself the "country" party in American politics, this transformation is potentially devastating.

George W. Bush and the Republican future

As president, George W. Bush has been at the center of debate over the future of the Republican Party. Until recently, Bush has maintained astronomical approval ratings among Republican voters, yet he has also charted a policy course for Republicans that much of the party has found disagreeable. He has led Republicans to the pinnacle of their post-Coolidge influence, but it is not yet clear whether he will actually leave his party in a stronger state than he found it for either the short or long terms.

Bush has bolstered some of the sources of party strength and undermined others. Clearly, he and Karl Rove have bolstered the technical superiority of Republicans. Bush has also promoted the institutionalization of conservatism, with strategic use of grants from the Department of Education and the National Endowment for the Humanities. The President has both benefited from and helped to nurture the "new media" with strategies designed to increase its access and prestige. Not least, in the wake of 9-11, Bush succeeded in mobilizing the crucial third leg of the Republican coalition, which was mostly dormant through the 1990s: nationalist-minded foreign policy hawks.

On the other side of the ledger, Bush has almost certainly undermined through negligence the critical task, carried out by Goldwater, Reagan, and Gingrich, of advancing a public argument that makes sense out of otherwise disparate concrete policy questions by connecting them to a broader philosophical framework. He has largely abandoned the philosophical argument for limited government that once defined the Republican Party, and has not succeeded in winning broad acceptance for the alternative of "compassionate conservatism" (or what some have called "big government conservatism"). To a large extent, he has abandoned the systematic promotion of public philosophy altogether.

As Republicans survey this picture and regroup, seven propositions should guide them.

Proposition #1: National security has to come first.

National security in an age of terror must be the first priority of any party responsible for administration of the national government. The consequences of failure could be catastrophic for the lives, liberty, and well-being of millions of Americans. Furthermore, the defense of the nation is one of the few tasks of the modern federal establishment that is actually firmly grounded in a constitutional mandate. If Americans get this issue wrong, nothing else will matter.

Politically, President Bush and congressional Republicans gained big dividends in 2002 and 2004 from the renewed prominence of national security issues and from their tough stand on those issues. Indeed, national security is the best single explanation for Bush's reelection and increased Republican congressional contingents since 2000, and it is one of the few issues on which Republicans have held the advantage in recent years in public perception. To lose this advantage would be perilous indeed.

Consequently, for both policy and political reasons, Republicans cannot afford to falter in the national security arena or to allow themselves to be outflanked by Democrats. There are a number of potential threats to Republican dominance of the national security area. Iraq may continue to erode public trust in the party's competence. If the President's policy of democratizing the Middle

East is framed in a manner that disconnects it from hard American national interest, it may lose the support of the group Richard Lowry of the *National Review* recently referred to as the "To-Hell-With-Them Hawks." And Republicans face a conundrum: If there is another terrorist attack on American soil, George Bush will be held responsible to a degree he was not on 9-11; if there is no attack, memories of 9-11 will continue fading and with them the sense of urgency about national security.

Consequently, Republicans must spare no effort to retain their national security *bona fides*, but they must also avoid becoming completely dependent on that issue. They must prepare for the day—or even the short-lived moment—when they will have to do better on domestic questions in order to win.

Proposition #2: Mobilization is not enough.

Bush's reluctance to engage in public argument in a sustained way may end up outweighing his more numerous but more technical contributions to his party. It is this vacuum which is arguably responsible for the Republicans' sense of philosophical malaise and for the related impression that Republicans now see power as an end in itself.

The minority—which almost describes Republicans today, and may actually describe them on November 8—cannot rely purely on mobilization. The majority, even when that majority is narrow, can be tempted to rely wholly on mobilization, since it seems that all one needs to do is win again where one prevailed before. The degree to which Bush relied on mobilizing the "base vote" in 2004 has often been exaggerated; in actuality, he improved his vote more among "blue voters" and in "blue states" than elsewhere, and won some crucial swing groups, like Catholics. Nevertheless, his general approach has downplayed public argument and teaching.

As a long term strategy, this choice has major flaws. For one thing, it cedes the high ground to anyone who actually offers a broad persuasive argument. Americans perceive today's high level of partisanship as connected to both parties' tendency to mobilize their supporters rather than reach beyond them. For another, it holds little promise of luring future voters. A strategy based primarily on mobilization operates as if the electorate is fixed. In reality, the electorate gradually loses members who can no longer be mobilized and gains new members who have not yet developed fixed loyalties.

Furthermore, for two reasons, Republicans as a party have more to lose than Democrats by failing to advance a public philosophy. First, because the benefits they offer usually promise concentrated gain and dispersed cost, it is easier for Democrats to assemble a coalition on the basis of material interest without direct reliance on a public philosophy. Second, the institutions primarily responsible for interpreting the world and conveying ideas to the public—the educational system, the mass media, and popular culture—largely perform the task of advancing liberalism for the Democrats. Although Republicans now have some alternative institutions and alternative media to promote an alternative argument, a larger part of the burden still rests on the party itself.

If there has indeed been a rolling Republican realignment, it rolled over a period of four decades in no small part because of the accumulated effects of an extensive effort at national persuasion. Reagan made a persistent argument, and now the 30–44 year-old age group which largely came of age during his presidency is one of the most Republican-leaning cohorts of American voters. There is thus far no evidence that the "Bush cohort" will imitate them, and in 2004, the youngest voters gave John Kerry his biggest margins. Reagan's oft-repeated vision of limited constitutional government played an important role in putting Chief Justice John Roberts and Justice Samuel Alito on their paths to the Supreme Court. It is far from clear that Bush is inspiring a next generation of conservative jurists who will be available to take their place in twenty-five years. It is ironic that Republicans have stopped making a concerted effort to shape the public philosophy at the very moment wide new channels of communication have become available for them in the new media. No Republican strategy can ignore the mobilization of Republican partisans, but first Republicans need partisans to mobilize. It has to be the goal of Republicans to break out of the current near-stalemate, in which they hold a meager and unsatisfying majority in the "51 percent nation," yet a strategy tilted away from public argument seems unlikely to yield such a breakout. Thus, Republicans need a strategy that relies on mobilization during elections and systematic persuasion between elections.

Proposition #3: Compassionate conservatism cannot be jettisoned in its entirety.

"Compassionate conservatism" has long been viewed skeptically by almost all liberals and many conservatives. The former have considered it oxymoronic, the latter insultingly redundant. Observers have long wondered whether it was best considered a governing philosophy, a political strategy, a campaign tactic, or all three. Today, the conservative debate over Bush and compassionate conservatism can be seen in the wildly different appraisals of Fred Barnes and Bruce Bartlett, in whose eyes it is either a bold innovation or a betrayal.[1]

In general, compassionate conservatism has meant de-emphasizing rhetoric of limited government, federalism, and other constitutional principles (except when discussing judicial appointments) and emphasizing policies aimed at appealing to targeted minorities while keeping the GOP's conservative base mostly intact. It has meant promising to mobilize what the President calls the "armies of compassion" of civil society. More specifically, it has meant large tax cuts without an accompanying drive for serious spending restraint, large new education and Medicare programs, and a general accommodation of big government linked to proposals enhancing accountability and choice. Bush's "ownership society" was to be an umbrella covering many of these choice features. Perhaps Republicans could co-opt big government, bend it to their purposes, and make it their friend. It has also included a firm adherence to social conservatism, though also a reluctance to trumpet it too loudly or too broadly. More generally, a key atmospheric element of compassionate conservatism has been Bush's reluctance to highlight issues like welfare reform and affirmative action that might threaten to put sharp edges back on the Republican project.

In its favor, it has been argued for "compassionate conservatism" that it succeeded in narrowing the gender gap, pulling up the GOP vote among blacks (by a bit) and Hispanics (by more), and softening the harsh reputation associated with (as Bill Clinton's reelection campaign put it so often) the "Gingrich-Dole Republicans" of the 1990s. It offered some forward strategy for Republicans who could not realistically expect to roll back big government very far, if at all. Limited government, it was argued, was by itself a sufficient doctrine for a minority party, but when Republicans attained a majority in government it left them bereft of options. Finally, while limited government conservatism delivered some smashing successes for Republicans at the presidential level in the 1980s and in Congress in 1994, it never succeeded in putting together the whole package in the way that compassionate conservatism can claim to have done in 2002 and 2004.

Whatever their misgivings, Republicans cannot jettison compassionate conservatism in its entirety, though the moniker will likely not survive. It was, after all, developed as a response to real strategic dilemmas. Republicans did need a positive agenda as a governing party, they did have to appeal better to women and to the fast-growing Hispanic population, and they did have to soften a rather harsh image that emerged from the 1990s. Most of these dilemmas have not gone away; for example, Republicans can hardly stop trying to appeal to Hispanics without writing off their future as a party.

Proposition #4: Although Republicans cannot throw overboard compassionate conservatism in its entirety, they cannot and should not try to retain it as the foundation of their future strategy.

Among presidential programs, compassionate conservatism most closely resembles in its strategic aims Dwight Eisenhower's "Modern Republicanism" and Bill Clinton's "New Covenant" by "New Democrats," other attempts by presidents to rub off the hard edges of their party's reputation by muting principles held by a majority within their party. These earlier examples do not bode well for Bush's experiment—while they met short-term political exigencies, neither Eisenhower's nor Clinton's projects demonstrated much staying power after the men left office.

The weaknesses of Bush's approach are clear. Perhaps foremost, whatever political burdens may come attached to a more vigorous defense of limited government, there were sound policy and political reasons that Republicans embraced that stand for decades prior to 2000. Certain objective realities make it important for at least one of the two major parties to carry the banner of limited government, and to do so rather openly. As the sclerotic European economies attest, excessive government spending, taxing, and regulating are objectively a prescription for a downward spiral of economic and social stagnation—a spiral that is politically quite difficult to break, let alone reverse.

It is notable that hardly anyone has promoted the package of compassionate conservatism as the best available policy; to put it another way, hardly anyone advocating compassionate conservatism has done so by attempting to demonstrate that limited government is no longer a preferable option from the standpoint of good policy. (Choice and accountability were offered as the next best thing to limited government, as realistic departures that could make liberal programs more conservative, but they have proven much less popular than advocates had expected and have been whittled down to a mere shadow in bill after bill.) Yet the starting point of policy should always be the question of what is best for the country. Indeed, Republicans have long maintained that good policy will ultimately be good politics, even if it is not always so in the short term. Translating that precept into terms of the current controversy, if Hayek, Friedman, Goldwater, and Reagan (not to mention the framers of the Constitution) have been invalidated—if the laws of economics and the laws of human nature have changed so that overweening centralized state power no longer poses a threat to prosperity, liberty, and civic virtue—then, by all means, the argument for limited government should be allowed to slide into disuse. If not, the party's task must be to find a way to make the argument more compelling. The corresponding political reality is that a very large proportion of Republican voters share that view and are not going to change it anytime soon.

Inattention to these realities has led to a number of political difficulties for Republicans. For one thing, compassionate conservatism has foreclosed the use of a number of hard-edged issues (like welfare reform reauthorization) that could have given Republicans considerable traction against recalcitrant Democrats. For another, it is probable that most Republicans never bought into "compassionate conservatism" as anything but a tactical device. As is often the case, opportunism brings its own punishment. Because voters are not stupid, and because there is a rough moral justice even in the world of politics, no party should ever adopt an approach that it does not actually believe in. Now Republicans are faced with responsibility for a number of policies that they find unpalatable and perhaps even indefensible but from which they find it impossible to retreat (the Medicare prescription drug entitlement is the best example). The loss of focus on limited government has likewise been blamed by commentators like Peggy Noonan for contributing to the slide of congressional Republicans into lobbying scams and other excesses.[2]

After allowing the spigots of domestic spending to flow freely since 1999—a trend pre-dating Bush—Republicans in Congress have bumped up against fiscal reality and have had to cut back, risking an election-year backlash. It would surely have been politically easier to exert greater fiscal discipline from the beginning. Increasing federal education funding by 20 percent would have posed fewer political difficulties than increasing it by 40 percent and then cutting it, even by a small amount. Without some consideration of first principles, it is hard for policymakers to critically evaluate or prioritize programs, which is a necessary prerequisite to constraining them.

In contrast, whatever the political difficulties, the only times that the growth of domestic government has significantly slowed have been times when Republicans pushed the limited government argument hardest—under Reagan and in the mid-1990s. The advocates of Bush's approach have argued, correctly, that no matter how hard they have tried, Republicans have never succeeded in substantially cutting back government. Critics respond, just as correctly, that when Republicans have tried hard to cut government, they have at least succeeded in slowing it; when they have not tried to cut it at all, it has run amok, whether under Democratic or Republican administrations. In any event, if it is difficult for Republicans to cut programs that Democrats have ballooned, it is both difficult and highly awkward for them to cut programs that have ballooned under their own stewardship. By surrendering the argument for limited government, compassionate conservatism has surrendered the field on an issue of fundamental importance to the character of the nation. Altogether, far from representing a victory of realism over ideology, it has often represented a victory of tactical spin over reality.

In his autobiography, Ronald Reagan properly derided the purism that disdained all compromise, saying "If you got seventy-five or eighty percent of what you were asking for, I say, you take it and fight for the rest later, and that's what I told these radical conservatives who never got used to it."[3] However, the policy and rhetorical mandates of compassionate conservatism have systematically pushed Bush toward deals in which he got neither enough good policy nor enough political payoff to justify what he gave up. Bush has also neglected the lesson that, on occasion, no loaf actually may be better than half a loaf or one-third of a loaf, especially if the loaf itself is indigestible; such occasions often offer invaluable opportunities for public teaching. Such criticisms, at any rate, seem plausible in the case of education, and more than plausible in the case of prescription drugs. In any game of negotiation, the starting point is quite important to the outcome. Bush's starting point on education and prescription drugs was itself a major concession, so the further compromises necessary to secure passage pulled the legislation even deeper into liberal territory. (In contrast, his 2003 tax cut was a real victory, despite being cut in half by Congress, because the starting point was strongly conservative and compromises left a bill that still significantly advanced Bush's cause).

Altogether, it seems unlikely that compassionate conservatism can carry the political weight assigned to it, or that limited government conservatism is the political loser that the advocates of compassionate conservatism hold it to be. The initial election of the Republican Congress in 1994 was owed to public rejection of the big government opening act of Bill Clinton's presidency and coincided with a strong limited government platform by the Republicans themselves. When the chips were down, Bush himself returned at critical junctures in the 2000 GOP primaries, the fall of 2000, and the fall of 2004 to a limited government, anti-big government theme. Bush performed better among Hispanics than did Reagan, but did worse among women. The gender gap may have been reduced in 2004 in comparison to 1996 or 2000, but Bush still narrowly lost the women's vote, and in any event his improved women's vote was probably due more to national security fears than to compassionate conservatism; in contrast, the more limited government-oriented Reagan actually *won* the women's vote in

1984, as did Bush's father in 1988 in a Reaganesque campaign. And, of course, Bush barely won reelection with 51 percent of the vote, thirty-one states, and 286 electoral votes; Reagan won reelection with 59 percent of the vote, forty-nine states, and 525 electoral votes. The circumstances were, of course, very different, as were the candidates, and this side-by-side comparison is much too simple. Nevertheless, it raises serious doubts about compassionate conservatism's electoral superiority, even in the short run.

Proposition #5: Republicans must preserve their alliance of social conservatives and economic conservatives.

Since the beginning of the Republican ascendancy, no Republican presidential candidate has succeeded without successfully appealing to the social conservatives alongside the economic conservatives. By deemphasizing limited government economic conservatism, compassionate conservatism arguably threatens the Republican coalition at this most basic level.

It has long been contended that the economic conservatives and social conservatives who have allied in the Republican camp are inherently hostile and on the verge of divorce. Indeed, *The New York Times* has predicted this divorce for so long that one can be forgiven for assuming that it is not a real possibility. However, there are clear tensions, which could lead to at least a trial separation, visible in the rising proportion of voters with incomes over $100,000 voting Democratic since 1996, presumably on cultural issues. While many are quick to blame this trend on Bush's social conservatism, it is more precise to say that it is due to the way Bush has allowed economic limited-government conservatism to atrophy relative to social conservatism. President Bush, well aware of his father's tale of woe, has given great attention to the tax issue. He almost certainly underestimated, however, the importance to a significant proportion of economically-conservative voters of spending control, deficit control, and persistent application of a rhetoric of limited government. Many "moderates" also find these dimensions of economic conservatism, rather than tax cuts, the most appealing.

Bush is arguably no more socially conservative than was Reagan, in policy or rhetoric. Even Goldwater, later touted as something of a libertarian, ran a socially conservative campaign in 1964, during which he gave a thirty-minute nationally-televised speech condemning the Supreme Court's recent decision banning prayer in public schools. But Bush's social conservatism stands out more because his limited-government conservatism stands out less. Ironically, this is a new version of the same problem Bush's father had in 1992, when he had to appeal so strongly to social conservatives because the 1990 tax increase had alienated so many economic conservatives. (The trial separation then took the form of flirtation with Ross Perot by voters who were fiscally conservative but socially moderate.) Additionally, one might speculate that swing voters feel less threatened by a socially-conservative party that is also explicitly a limited-government party; the latter feature puts the former feature into a more temperate context.

Both the Bush approach and its opposite—the view, widely heralded in the mainstream media, that the GOP would do well to cut loose the social conservatives—fail to account for an important fact. A very large number of Republican voters are both limited-government *and* social conservatives—perhaps more than are in either group alone. A strategy that deliberately undercuts either side of that equation not only alienates those who are unadulterated devotees of one of the two wings, but reduces by 50 percent the affection for their party held by the group that professes both principles, leaving them adrift and vulnerable to capture on an *ad hoc* basis by a particularly agile Democrat.

That so many of the party's voters are both limited-government and social conservatives gives a clue to how the party can keep its two wings together: Social conservatism can and should be defended as a necessary concomitant to the maintenance of free society. One of Ronald Reagan's great talents was arguing for the socially conservative position on family and religion by asserting the centrality of those institutions to the moral infrastructure of a system of freedom and limited government. This argument can be made on issues as controversial as abortion, same-sex marriage, and embryonic stem-cell research—but only if Republicans adopt a strategy of persuasion mixed with mobilization rather than simply mobilizing by "preaching to the choir."

Proposition #6: It is possible to imagine a politically-attractive amalgam of compassionate conservatism and limited-government conservatism.

Although they differ in spirit and rhetorical direction, there are numerous specific pieces that are a part of both visions, including support for tax cuts, privatization and choice provisions in a number of government programs, voluntarism, and an alliance with social conservatism. One might say that compassionate conservatism is limited-government conservatism minus fiscal restraint, constitutionalist rhetoric, and a certain insouciance toward politically correct shibboleths.

There is no reason why a Republican strategy could not combine some features of compassionate conservatism with a more traditional focus on limited government, relying on the genuine convictions of most Republicans yet attending to some of the concerns that led to the rise of Bush's alternative. Such an approach might include:

❖ Holding the fiscal line, supporting both tax cuts and a serious, hard-headed effort at spending restraint summarized by the motto "first, do no harm"—that is, control the programs that exist and do not create new ones

❖ Re-energizing a public discourse of constitutionalism, limited government and federalism, and with it a renewed emphasis on persuasion, argument, and the forging of a public philosophy

❖ Supporting a measured cultural traditionalism as an essential component of the Republican package, framed as preserving the moral infrastructure of free society

❖ Introducing mechanisms for greater choice and accountability in existing public programs, including some version of the "ownership society," though being more sensitive to the practical and political limitations of choice

❖ Concerted campaigning in the black and Hispanic communities on the basis of cultural values and entrepreneurship

❖ Embracing legal immigration while insisting on assimilation and the promotion of American nationality

❖ Continuing to promote the vitality of civil society

❖ Thinking seriously of ways to institutionalize or operationalize the doctrine of limited government to make it a more viable doctrine for a governing party. For example, it might be time to resurrect a version of Lamar Alexander's 1996 promise to "cut their pay and send them home" by limiting the length of the congressional session. The party could restore budget targets, sequestrations, and pay-as-you-go rules for new spending. It could establish a concrete goal of reducing the percentage of GDP taken up by federal spending or pushing back the date on which the average American finishes paying his share of federal revenue, spending, and/or regulatory costs

❖ In foreign policy, insisting on a strong defense, strong presidential powers to deal with foreign threats, the assertion of national sovereignty, an offensive forward strategy against terrorism and its state supporters, and efforts to reach the root of the problem by promoting reform in the Middle East—all proposed and defended on grounds of American national interest, broadly conceived

Such a mix can serve as a program for Republicans as either the majority or minority. The principle of no (or few) new programs and restrained spending on old ones is essentially negative in character; application of the "ownership society" to existing big government is essentially positive and active in character. While this outline eschews much of what makes Bush's message unique, it can do so without sacrificing any of the more technical advances under his watch.

Consistent presidential leadership is vital for the fullest execution of this (or any other) platform. As we have seen, without that leadership, even a Republican Congress is overtaken with the seductions of power; with it, Congress might be directed or, failing that, disciplined with the veto and the bully pulpit. The importance of presidential leadership can be seen in the high levels of public support for two presidents whose appropriation vetoes led to government shutdowns. In the more famous case, Bill Clinton confronted the 104th Congress, attacked it for cutting government too much, allowed the government to shut down, and won the battle for public opinion. In the other case, Ronald Reagan confronted Congress in the early 1980s, attacked it for spending too much, allowed the government to shut down, and won the battle for public opinion.

Proposition #7: There are three key long-term challenges to the demographics of future Republican success which Republicans will need to address forcefully.

Working to the Republicans' benefit, they are considerably more likely to be married, have children, and have a large number of children than are Democrats. All other things being equal, Republicans have more babies, and consequently enjoy the prospect of building a long-term voter advantage over Democrats.

However, there are three potentially mortal challenges to that outcome which call for creative long-range thinking by Republicans. First, Democrats can seek to negate the Republican baby advantage by conversion accomplished through continued liberal control over the nation's public school system and its provision of higher education. Republicans abet this process of conversion when they neglect the task of advancing a public philosophy. They will also need to think about how best to undermine or bypass liberal dominance of education.

Second, Democrats may also offset the GOP baby bonus through immigration, an issue on which Republicans face a serious divide. If Republicans do nothing, they leave room for a third party to take up the cudgel and drain votes away; in any event, raising the Republican vote from 35 percent of Hispanics to 45 percent will still be a net loser if the total number of Hispanics continues to accelerate. If Republicans pursue a policy (or rhetoric) that is too restrictionist, it will alienate the large Mexican-American community, perhaps for decades. If Republicans embrace massive immigration without insisting on strict standards for citizenship, a crackdown on voter fraud, and a renewed emphasis on assimilation, they may be committing not only partisan but national suicide. If they do insist, they will doubtless be accused of "racism" by the mavens of multiculturalism, a risk old-fashioned conservatism might be willing to take but compassionate conservatism will not.

Third, as the population ages, efforts to restrain entitlement spending will be increasingly risky. Democrats are in the enviable position of being able to simply run the clock out, blocking reform until the only solution will appear to be a massive last-minute tax increase that will bring the United States much closer to European levels of taxing and spending. If Republicans do nothing, they will forfeit the 100-year match over whether America would ultimately succumb to social democracy. If they propose serious action to prevent that outcome, they run the risk of decisively losing the gigantic cohort of voters dependent on those programs.

Conclusion

Any discussion of future strategy for the parties is always subject to the vagaries of history. No one writing a paper like this on September 10, 2001 would have argued for focusing first on national security. One can nevertheless trace the outlines of probable challenges and possible responses. The combination of limited government, cultural traditionalism, and a strong defense has served Republicans well for the last four decades, and no alternative has been offered that seems superior, either in terms of policy or politics. The Republicans' task will be to revivify those principles, perhaps complement (though not replace) them, and apply them to new situations.

Roundtable Discussion

Michael Barone: We're at this conference at an interesting moment in our political history on our political calendar. The Democrats, at the moment, do not have a single national leader. I think perhaps aside from a reference to the New Zealand mountain area, I did not hear the name Hillary this morning, very much. Republicans are about to get new leaders. In three years' time George W. Bush won't be President, and in one year's time Bill Frist will not be Senate Majority Leader. Denny Hastert, current Speaker of the House, will probably retire in 2008, and there will either be a new Republican President or a failed Republican nominee as the nominal leader of the party. So we're thinking about the parties at a time when we're facing a short run where they seem not likely to be defined by current leaders, as much as they are.

We're also at a moment when the Republican Party, as Andy noted in the beginning of his remarks, is in some ways in a strong position. For many of us who have been watching the political scene for many years, the Republican capture of the majority in the House in 1994 seems like just a short time ago, but in fact, if you look at it historically, the Republicans are now, in terms of years of controlling the House, in their third longest period in the majority, exceeded only by the two from 1860 to 1874 and 1894 to 1910. It is unusual in American history, and those of us who got used to forty years of Democratic control sometimes fail to understand this, but it is unusual in American history for any party to control the House for twelve years. It happens less often than not, so we are at a period where the problem of staleness that a party in control tends to have is a problem for the Republican Party.

When I look back on politics, over the period that I've been writing about it, which goes back more or less forty years, the biggest change in the Republican Party that strikes me, is that it's not obviously a minority party as it was forty years ago, but it is also becoming a more demotic people, a party of the people, a party that is more populist, more vulgar, and less of an elitist party. If you go back to the 1930s of the *New Yorker* cartoons, Republicans and the culture of that time were the snobs. They were the elegant ladies in their fancy outfits going to the opera, the snooty rich people that looked down on everyone else. That was the sort of image of the Republican Party.

Today I think it's really rather the opposite. The snobbery is mostly on the other side. Ronald Reagan brought to the Presidency and brought to the Republican Party a leader who echoed the universally appealing popular cultures from which he had made his living all of his life—radio in the 1920s and '30s, movies—the great movies of the 1930s and '40s—television in the 1950s. Those were universal media, and that's one of the things that enabled him to carry forty-nine states when he ran for re-election, and to carry forty-four when he was running against an incumbent President. It was universal appeal of a sort that's really not imaginable at this moment for a candidate for either party today.

George W. Bush grew up as a baby boomer, but our popular culture has moved away from the universal popular culture where the whole family went to the movies on the weekend, or the whole family sat watching the same TV show, where there certainly weren't any vulgar words. We have moved to niche media. Everyone's got their own TV, their own iPod, you're watching your own culture. And in that setting Bush represents a certain set of cultural attitudes that make him a positive and accessible figure for many Americans, and an utterly repulsive one for many others. And I think that much of the polarization and bitterness in our political life, which I think is a genuine factor, owes itself to something in the nature of happenstance occurrences. The fact is that our last two presidents are two baby boom presidents—Bill Clinton and George W. Bush, and both happen to have personal qualities that people on the other side of the cultural divide absolutely loathe. I mean, I don't think I have to go into any detail about that. You have to be a pretty strong partisan to avoid being able to see how both of these men are intensely polarizing. And then we had the 2000 election and the Florida controversy, and I think that particularly exacerbated it because both parties for strictly tactical reasons, I think, made arguments that happened to be congruent with their broader philosophies. I mean, the Democrats were saying the rules are unfair, change the rules, and that has been the Democrats' response every four years to losing presidential elections—let's change the rules for selecting him, make them fairer.

The Republicans' response was it's unfair to change the rules in the middle of the game—enforce the rules. And that was the subtext of the legal arguments at almost every stage in every one of the sixty-seven counties that we watched with such trepidation during that period. And obviously, for many Democrats, George W. Bush has not been and is not now a legitimate president. I think all of these things contribute to it. But the Republican Party has become in some sense the more populist party—the one that's more in touch with a wider segment of ordinary people. The Democratic Party, increasingly, is the party of elites and the media, university and, indeed, even corporate elites in our times. This is, in some ways, a problem for the Republican Party. During much of his presidency, George W. Bush's most effective opposition has not come from the Democratic Party or the Democratic politicians, but from *The New York Times,* CBS, ABC, NBC, and so forth. But that is a factor that he has also been able to overcome in the 2004 election, particularly.

Let me just note one other thing when I say the Republicans are a demotic party. A number of other things about the 2004 election, as I mentioned in my question to Michael Malbin this morning, I think came as a surprise to most Washington observers, including me. I thought the Republicans would out-raise the Democrats' in money. It turned out the Democrats, if anything, raised slightly more, or were roughly equal. We thought a number of things. One of the things we thought is if there's a big surge in turnout that will help the Democrats and elect a Democratic nominee. That was the assumption. Well, we got a chance to test that. There was a big surge in turnout and it elected the Republican nominee. John Kerry, many of you will remember, got 16 percent more popular votes than Al Gore. That's a big increase, and it's unusual in American history if you go down the election results comparing the turnout of the popular votes for the candidates from election to election. George W. Bush got 23 percent more votes in 2004 than he got in 2000. That's a huge increase. That's comparable to the 22 percent popular vote increase for Franklin Roosevelt between 1932 and 1936. It's historically highly unusual, and as the political philosopher James Carville said, "Where did all those Republicans come from?" The answer is, I think we're not sure about that, and we're not sure how it's going to play out in '06. The exit polls, as adjusted, showed party identification at 37/37. That's the best for Republican Party identification since random sample polling was started by Dr. Gallup in 1935.

The current public opinion polls, which are capturing not voters or likely voters, but all adults, show Democrats with a ten point advantage. Does that mean that the electorate has changed its mind and become less Republican? Does that mean that the polls are not sampling adequately the people who will turn out? I think that's really the very big question for the '06 election. Republicans now have a slightly larger reservoir of proven voters to draw on, to try and turn out in the off year, but there are also some reasons for thinking, and some other speakers have alluded to them, that Republican-based voters may be discouraged and less likely to turn out in '06. That's a question we don't know.

Let me just say a couple of things about national security, economic and cultural issues. On national security, we've heard a number of speakers talk this morning about a time when America has been under attack. That's obviously important. If you go back in history, Democrats had the advantage on national security issues from the 1940s to the 1960s. Franklin Roosevelt won on national security in 1940. If you'll look at the vote for other offices in the polling data, he would have lost if it was purely on domestic issues. Harry Truman's '48 victory owed a lot to the Berlin blockade and the success that we had in stopping the Communists from going into Berlin, and I think there's some polling evidence for that. Democrats suffered in '52 when they couldn't produce victory in Korea, but by 1960 John Kennedy is calling for more defense spending and a tougher defense policy against Fidel Castro than Richard Nixon. That was an advantage for the Democrats. Since the late '60s it has tended to be an advantage for Republicans. I think it will likely continue to be so, if only because I think Democrats are fundamentally split, not just on defense issues, but on the basic quality of American exceptionalism.

Is this a special or different country? Are we an especially good country? In 2004 Scott Rasmussen, pollster, asked voters a couple of questions about American exceptionalism: "Is this basically a fair and decent country or not? Would the world be better off if other countries were more like America or not?" What he found was that about two-thirds of American voters answered, "Yes," to both questions, as would Franklin Roosevelt, John Kennedy, Harry Truman, and so forth. Ninety percent of Republicans answered "Yes," to both questions. Among Democrats the margins were something in the nature of 47 to 39 percent. Well, that's a vote for American exceptionalism that reminds me of the story of the Teamsters' business agent who was at the hospital and got a bouquet of flowers with a note attached that said, "The executive board wishes you a speedy recovery by a vote of nine to six." It is not a wholehearted vote, and I think that continues to be a disadvantage for Democrats. I think we saw that play out in the '03, '04 cycle. Remember when John Kerry said I did actually vote for the eighty-seven billion dollars before I voted against it, he was in some sense acting rationally for a man who is a candidate of a party with two different constituencies, both of which he wanted to rally to the polls, so he gave one of them one vote, and one of them another. It wasn't a totally accidental statement. It reflected a weakness—not necessarily a fatal weakness—but a weakness of the party.

On economic issues, Andrew Busch has talked about compassionate conservatism. I prefer to see the Bush policies as having a reasonably coherent common thread of the idea of not making government smaller in some ways, or in making it larger, but introducing elements of choice and accountability. And as Andrew says, I think the jury is out whether that is going to be popular, whether that is going to be successful. I think it moves us in the direction that society has moved, that the private sector has moved over the years. We're seeing some of this play out in the Medicare Part D. You can get dueling polls on whether this is a great fiasco or a great success. I don't feel I know the final answer on that.

On healthcare policy we heard a number of policies, not all of which I'm sure I understand, from Elaine Kamarck. Perhaps I'm just not reading her clearly enough. But I think one of the things that may be happening as a result of the Medicare prescription drug bill, which the Republicans pushed through with a three-hour roll call in 2003 in the House of Representatives, is the Health Savings Account movement—a movement for more market measured health insurance policy. It seems to me that this has the potential to change the healthcare finance sector of our society in the way that a little known section of the Tax Reform Act of 1978 changed the private pension sector—that's 401K. Basically, that was little noticed at the time. It turned out to have profound implications, as others have noted—Elaine mentioned it in her speech—we have moved from a defined benefit pension to a defined contribution pension country. She is worried that some people will not take care of themselves well enough or be covered by the defined contribution. I would just say that when you have a defined benefit, it's all very nice to have it defined, but if General Motors goes belly up, you don't get the benefit. And we're watching that work out with some human cost in Michigan this year as we have with people who thought they were covered by LTV Steel and by United Airlines, and other things. It's nice to give people guarantees, but if you don't have the mechanism to deliver on those guarantees, you can cause people some problems.

Finally, on our cultural issues. America, in some ways, is becoming a slightly more moralistic society, or at least one in which behavior that many would consider immoral or dysfunctional is decreasing. Abortion, divorce, unwed birth, crime, welfare dependency are all on a decline. For some of those, some of the political actors, many of them Republicans but some of them Democrats, as well, can claim some credit, perhaps. I think also we're seeing changes in behavior. I think it's been an assumption among cultural liberals that you'll never get them back on the farm once they've seen Paris. They're having so much fun with this culturally liberal behavior that everybody will just want to behave that way forever and ever. It turns out the dynamics are somewhat different. On the one hand, we're not going back to the 1950s in many respects, you know, whether it's women not working outside the home (although the number of mothers with small children working outside the home is declining somewhat) or treatment of gays as they were in the 1950s. We aren't going back to that, but Paris doesn't look so good to some people. Children of divorced parents say they don't want to get divorced. The children very rarely vote for a divorce. That is one explanation, I think, of the fact that the number of divorces has been declining. And on demographics, Ruy Teixeira and I have sort of fenced off here, at least with considerable respect on my part for his work. I hope I have indicated that. And there are demographic trends that work in the direction of both parties.

Let me just conclude with one that tends to work out to the benefit of the Republican Party. Ninety-seven of the 100 fastest growing counties in the United States—and that's whether you measure 2000 to '03, 2000 to '04, 2000 to '05—voted for George W. Bush in 2004. Three of them voted for John Kerry, including Clark County, Nevada, which includes Las Vegas. As Ruy points out, those counties do not cast nearly as large a number of votes as the currently hundred largest counties in the United States, which are heavily Democratic margins on the whole, although some of those hundred largest are losing population at a considerable rate. I mean, San Francisco in the five years of this century has lost five percent of its population—an interesting fact. It has to do with the dog pound boom, I think, as well as conditions of life in San Francisco. Nonetheless, those hundred fastest growing counties did have 26 percent of the population growth in the United States between 2000 and 2005. Some of them are in states that are either heavily Republican or heavily Democratic. They're not likely to make a difference, but in the long run I think we are going to see, sooner or later, a change in the voting contours and voting patterns that have been pretty unchanging for ten years, from 1996 through 2004. I think we'll get changes as a result of 2008 nominees, quite possibly. We are not always going to always see elections that look very close to mirror images of the others. In that context I think the Republican Party has its problems, but also has its strengths. Thank you.

Hugh Hewitt: On election eve, 2004, November 1st, John Kerry was in courthouse square in Warren, Ohio. I knew then that George Bush would be reelected, because he would carry Ohio, because if you have to campaign in the steel valley of the Mahoning and Trumbull counties around Warren Ohio, and you're a Democratic nominee on election night, you've lost. But I actually confirmed that two months earlier, July 4th, when I was back in Warren, which is my hometown, with my brother and his family and his five sisters-in-law. They were all gathered around, all of whom had gone to John F. Kennedy High

School as I did (the Roman Catholic high school), all of whom had many, many children, all of whom were there talking politics, and not one of them was going to vote for John Kerry. They were the product of a union household, they were all Catholic, they were all mothers, and they were all married, and not one of them was going to vote for John Kerry.

I have thought about that since, and it is really the dilemma the Democratic Party faces and the advantage the Republican Party faces, and that is that the Republican Party is the party of certainty, and the Democratic Party is not. We are certain about the six things that Professor Busch talked about, but primarily about national security and primarily about the proposition that Michael referred to, that America is a great and good country and, in fact, that which it stands for, both in the global war on terror and in its general day-to-day life are great things that ought to be honored, and there is less conviction about that in the Democratic Party and often opposition to it. I always have to add I am not questioning anyone's patriotism here, I'm simply talking about how it appears to the average American that the Democratic Party thinks about this country and about the value of what they do, particularly their faith lives, and particularly the value of their work.

I want to talk about the pros and the cons that the Republicans face going forward. They've built off of what Professor Busch said, but I think they are really, really quite significant if you study them very closely. The first is that in the new communications era with new media—talk radio, especially the blogosphere, but also the Fox News Channel and the variety of new ways of communicating—the Republican Party has developed a bench that is deep and is also imbued with rectitude. It is not profane, it is not vulgar, and it is not cruel. But unfortunately, for the Democratic Party, at the time that the new media exploded, which was just about the time of the Florida fiasco, there was a tremendous amount of anger in the Democratic Party—a tremendous amount of resentment, and a tremendous amount of feeling that they had been cheated—and that translated into a generation of Democratic Party activists who are not skilled in polemics, who are not skilled in communication, and who have, in fact, abandoned themselves to an excess that scares middle America a great deal.

It's not often you'll find a Congressman [Timothy] Roemer representing the Democratic Party on television. You will find, instead, a number of people who say extraordinarily difficult things for ordinary Americans to absorb. For example, yesterday when the President appeared in a town hall meeting in North Carolina, he was confronted by a questioner who said, "You are tapping my phone. You are taking me away without trial for years at a time." And he went on a litany and he concluded, "I have never been as afraid today as I have ever been in my life about living in this country." Well, if you think about that, that is patently absurd, because most people simply do not identify with that. As Matthew Dowd, presidential strategist, said, "If you can connect at a level of values with people and make them understand that you feel what they feel, then you will win their votes." George W. Bush has done that successfully in election cycles, less successfully over the last year, but he is returning to it again, and that rectitude, that ordinary ability to communicate, and the friendliness that goes, I think, primarily on the center right now is a decided advantage.

The second advantage is Grace. Listen very closely to Congressman Roemer talk about his family and five-year-old Grace. I don't believe any parent is ever happier than the least happy of their children. And as these generational politics take over, married couples with children voted an overwhelmingly significant advantage for George W. Bush in 2004. And as a result, those people are going to bring up their children with an eye to voting their future, and if they are uncertain about the Democratic Party's view on the core goodness of the West, if they're worried about what will Grace be doing in twenty years and in twenty-five years, they're going to tend to vote Republican, with a couple of quick cautions.

First off, those are the two great advantages that Republicans have, and they were touched upon in the cultural conservatism critique that Professor Busch offered, but there are two very deep, troubling aspects. One is the temptation of nativism. Bill wrote about this just last week, and it's something I wrote in the new book. It is something that alarms me—that in this debate about immigration, there is an abandonment of the principles of Reagan. Now, Reagan did believe in border control, and I believe in border control, but there is a tinge that could grow very, very quickly into the fiasco of Prop 187 in California here in 1994, in which we saw a generation of Latinos decide that the Republican Party could never represent them in this state. And as a result, with the exception of the recall, which was an extraordinary circumstance, no significant statewide race has been won by a Republican candidate since 1994. Short-term gain, long-term not pain, but disaster for the Republican Party, because it became nativist, and it is so tempting to go there. It will not work in the long haul, and the Democratic Party can be counted on, I think, to look at two things from the 2000 census and the 2004 election. Ten million African-Americans who were eligible to vote did not vote in 2004. Eight million Latino Americans who were eligible to vote did not vote in 2004. George Bush beat John Kerry by three million votes. Do the math. If the American public, especially the emerging populations, conclude that the Republican Party is itself elitist and anti-immigrant, will lose the significant long-term advantages that Professor Busch talked about and that Michael underlined.

The second disadvantage, I think, is a cultural critique, which I hear echoes of from the 1980s. How many of you know the name Gordon Gecko? Okay, it's vanishing, but there came an attitude in the '80s that Michael Douglas exemplified in the movie *Wall Street* of Gordon Gecko. It was used as a critique and a cudgel on Republicans for a good ten years. It was the decade of greed. It was the party of excess. I'm not talking about Abramoff. I'm not talking about Duke Cunningham. I'm talking about a very coarse culture that is yet to be assigned to the Republicans, but as I was talking with Bill and with our students at lunch, the episode at Duke has me very, very, very troubled, not because it's unique—it isn't.

In 1976, when I was an undergrad and Bill was a teacher at Harvard, the Harvard football team went down to the combat zone and their quarterback was killed, accosting a prostitute when the pimp got involved in it. It's not like young men don't do stupid things. However, the coarseness of this [Duke episode] is a rather un-remarked upon quality. You combine it with the MySpace horror stories, the Facebook horror stories, and the stings that Dateline is doing, and you understand that there is a deep, deep sickness in the culture that is not being remedied by whatever the overt religiosity of the culture of compassion is. If and when the Democratic Party can critique what it is about that and assign it to the Republican Party, I think they'll have a pretty, pretty significant advantage.

In the new book that I wrote, the blocking and tackling of 2006 is, I think, not very difficult. The Republicans have four messages: Win the war, confirm the judges, cut the taxes, control the spending. It's pretty easy. It's twelve words. They can, with significant repetition and positioning, drive that home. Moreover, if they make the war the central issue in 2006, I believe that on the war there is no serious argument that the Democrats can be trusted to prosecute it. In fact, if you believe John Murtha, and I do, if you believe Nancy Pelosi, and I do, if you believe Russ Feingold, and I do, Democrats think that the President is a criminal who violated the Constitution and we ought to get out of Iraq immediately. That's why I think the campaign of 2006 will be a referendum on those very propositions, and I think, once again, intuitively the American people know, and they will be reminded shortly with the debut of United 93, if they have forgotten. I don't think they have. They know that the war is a very serious thing. It's an existential threat. But for a few lucky breaks on 9-11, we would not have had merely a massacre, but a decapitation and a republic-changing event. As Mark Steyn said on my program yesterday, "All of the agencies failed, but thank God for Todd Beamer and his friends aboard United 93, ordinary Americans who understood what they had to do." That still matters a great deal to America. It still remains. A text, a long time ago that I read, said that the West will never be in crisis, even if it is defeated, if it remains confident of what it stands for, if it has certainty about its purposefulness and its virtue.

The Republican Party still has that certainty. It was, in fact, what powered Ronald Reagan. It is what, I think, powers George W. Bush—a certainty about what they are about and the goodness of the country. I think the Democrats are befuddled on that. I know Peter Beinart's new book is making the argument we've got to go back to Truman days, but unless and until they successfully purge the Michael Moore element from their party—which was welcomed in the Presidential box at the Democratic Convention in 2004 by President Carter— unless and until they purge the moveon.org excess, unless and until they take the advantage of perhaps the most prophetic piece that I would recommend to you, they will fail. From Soxblog, Dean Barnett is a writer who writes for Bill's magazine quite frequently on the online edition, and he wrote a letter to a young blogger, which I quote extensively in the new book, because it's so remarkably on point. He lectures a young leftist that in order to persuade Americans to your side you actually have to allow them into your living room. You have to be able to engage them and have them listen to you. Until the Democratic Party abandons that almost vicious edge that it developed while in its wilderness years, it will remain in the wilderness and the Republicans will have that permanent majority. Thank you.

William Kristol: I want to make four observations on the state of the parties—four empirical observations, which cut in slightly different directions, and you can decide what they end up amounting to.

First of all, it's pretty obvious that there has been a change in the relative status of the two parties. From '32 to '68 we had the New Deal System, and Democrats were almost entirely dominant, having controlled the presidency all those years, except for Eisenhower, and the Congress for all those years but four, I believe, when the New Deal coalition fell apart in '68 under the pressure of Vietnam and urban riots. Johnson got more than 60 percent of the presidential vote in 1964. But four years later, in 1968, the Democratic candidate received only 42 percent—one of the most precipitous falls in American history—and Nixon/Wallace got the rest of the vote. Then between 1968 and 2004, I would say, we have a 36-year-period of a rolling Republican realignment. Reagan wins in '80, bringing in a Republican Senate. The Republicans lose the Senate in '86, and finally lose the presidency in '92. With the end of the Cold War, and foreign policy and national security receding as an issue, Perot shows up, the first Bush collapses, and Clinton wins. But then in '94, for the first time in 40 years, Republicans gain control of both Houses of Congress, which they've maintained since, with the brief exception of the Jeffords switch, which caused the Democrats to control the Senate in the last half of 2001 and 2002. In 2004, the Republican president was reelected, while Republicans increased their seats in both houses of Congress at the same time that Bush increased his margin (or created a margin in the popular vote for the first time).

That is the big picture: Republicans gaining parity, and a slight edge now, over the Democrats after having been way, way down in either '30 or '34 or, for that matter, in '64, after the Goldwater debacle. It doesn't mean Republicans win every election, obviously. Democrats lost elections even during their heyday. It doesn't mean that the slogan "Had enough?" isn't still effective. (I'm glad Newt Gingrich is now writing Democratic talking points—though, maybe that's a sign of slight intellectual weakness in the Democratic Party. No offense to Newt, but the Democrats should really develop their own slogans.) In fact, if Democrats run on "Had enough?" this fall, they might take back the House, and they might pick up Senate seats. It's hard to govern if you control both branches of government. You don't get credit for what goes well, especially if you're as incompetent at taking credit for what's gone well as the Bush administration is. To have the kind of economic performance we've had since 9-11, which is pretty spectacular, the best in the Western world, exceeding all expectations—4.7 percent unemployment, 4 percent annual growth—and for people to think by a margin of two to one that Bush is doing a bad job on the economy is a pretty impressive feat by the White House and the Secretary of the Treasury, among others.

So you could have a bad mid-term election this year. I rather think we will. Tim Roemer mentioned that the slogan "Had enough?" comes from 1946, and this year could be like 1946. That was a bad mid-term election for the Democrats. They had been in power for twelve years, controlling both the presidency and Congress. People were tired of them. The election outcome was a negative verdict, a "time for a change" kind of verdict. But what did it mean beyond that? It meant nothing—certainly not that the Democrats had been rejected in any profound and lasting way. In fact, the Democrats won the presidency two years later and continued to control American politics for the next two decades. So I don't think Democrats should be too cheered up by the notion that they're going to run a "Had enough?" campaign in 2006 and win. They could do that and still see the Republicans hold onto the presidency in 2008.

The truth is, if the Democrats win the House, that will make it more likely that Republicans will win the presidency in 2008, not less. I honestly believe that. Not much important legislation will come out of the House in the next two years, so I would just as soon see Nancy Pelosi as Speaker and Charlie Rangel as Chairman of Ways and Means seeking to raise your taxes every day. John Conyers as Chairman of Judiciary—that would be excellent. Alcee Hastings, the impeached Federal Judge, as Chairman of the Intelligence Committee. The most moderate Democratic committee chairman would be Barney Frank on the Banking Committee. So as a Republican, I wouldn't mind letting the voters take a look at the Democratic Party as it runs the House for the next year and a half, going into 2008.

The single most likely scenario, if you look at the big trend, is that the Democrats will pick up the House, maybe narrowly, or almost pick it up. The Senate, I think, will be different. Voters get to know Senate candidates, and tend to make candidate-specific determinations, in ways they don't usually in House races, especially if there's a national wave. Republicans, one hopes, will hold the Senate, so they can confirm Supreme Court Justices. Then in 2008, if you look at the match-ups, it's amazing. Bush is weak now, and Republicans are getting clobbered in the generic congressional ballot in '06. But if you match up the two Republican candidates who are leading in Republican primary polls, McCain and Giuliani, against Hillary Clinton, who is leading in the Democratic polls, the Republicans win easily in 2008.

It's useful in politics sometimes to be simple-minded. The simple-minded take on the data is that the Democrats will do well in 2006, and the Republicans will win the presidential election in 2008, which would be consistent with the general trend of realignment in a Republican direction—interrupted, much as the Democratic realignment was once interrupted, by a little bit of "Had enough?" sentiment in an off-year election. So that's number one: general realignment in a Republican direction.

Number two is the stability of the last decade. From '96 to 2004 we've had an amazingly stable political situation. Michael Barone alluded to this: very even races every year from '96 to 2004—with very little deviation in the national congressional vote, though a slight Republican trend. The Republicans held the majority by a slight edge. If you look at the Democratic vote for the Presidency, Clinton got 49 percent plus in 1996, Gore got roughly 48.5 percent in 2000, and Kerry got 48 point something in 2004—so a very stable electoral situation. That is a fact that could last.

Generally, though, history would suggest that these things break apart at some point, and I think they most likely will, maybe in 2006–2008, maybe shortly after that. One reason to think the pattern might break up sooner rather than later is the huge surge in turnout that Barone referred to in 2004. Generally speaking, big increases in turnout lead to volatility and movement in the relationship between the parties, and it stands to reason. It's not an accident that the '94 Republican victory came two years after '92—the only (I think) other election in the last thirty years when there has been an uptick in turnout, which has been declining since the late '60s. Clinton and Perot got people to the polls. There were a lot of Perot voters, in particular, who were more or less unattached in '94. Gingrich did a good job of reaching out to them. Clinton, with the health-care plan, the tax increase, and his problems with the military, didn't do a very good job, and Republicans had a huge surge in the off-year elections of '94.

So I think the odds are that the stability of the period 1996 to 2004 breaks up at some point, and we get increased volatility in the electorate. But maybe not. Maybe the stability will continue another twenty years. It's a highly polarized country. The red state-blue state balance is roughly even, and there are some countervailing demographic forces. We might be meeting ten years from now and still have a sort of 51–49 country. It's hard to say. But analytically, a question to think about is, are the odds greater for continued stability or for the thing breaking one way or another?

Number three is 9-11: I think 9-11's impact has been underestimated throughout this day—maybe because it's a conference on the parties, and 9-11 is tangential to the relationship between the two political parties, which is a political and domestic matter, not a world politics matter. But you can't have as big a shock as 9-11, and as big a change in world politics, international politics, and American foreign policy as 9-11 produced, I think, without it affecting the parties themselves, as well as the relations between them. I think when historians look back at the last fifty or sixty years, they will say there was the Cold War era followed by the '90s, the decade of peace and prosperity—false peace in some ways, but still. The '90s ended on September 11, 2001, and we're now in a new era.

One characteristic of a new era is volatility and unpredictability, both in the world (and we've had a lot of that) and at home. If you want a comparison, look at the early years of the Cold War, with the volatility of the '46 election, a big Republican victory, then the huge Truman comeback in '48. By '52 Truman is incredibly unpopular again and can't even run for reelection. Then Joe McCarthy appears, we see bitter domestic politics, huge splits within the Democratic Party, Truman challenged in the '48 election by Henry Wallace and Strom Thurmond, both defectors from his own party—an incumbent challenged by two defectors in a general election. And on the other side there's Dewey vs. Taft, Eisenhower vs. Taft, and very deep rifts within the Republican Party.

That feels, to me, like the politics we're going through—a little bit suppressed, I would say, by the fact that we were attacked directly, and there was a certain rallying and uniting, first of the country and then, at least, of the Republicans. With Kerry in 2004 we see a desire to beat Bush, so a certain muting of differences among the Democrats—Dean on the one hand, Lieberman on the other. Kerry straddles the party and gets the nomination. So I think, in a way, the shock of 9-11 has been muted over the last year, but it will continue reverberating through the political system. It's very hard to know how that plays out. Of course, everything depends on what happens in the world, but I disagree with Andy Busch that 9-11 is fading as an issue.

We're going to have, in 2008, the first presidential election since '68 when American troops are deployed abroad and fighting, and probably engaged in pretty serious fighting against an insurgency, with Iran still a clear and present threat. Maybe Iran will have been dealt with, maybe not, but in either case, there will be the possibility of the most radical regime in the most dangerous part of the world, with unquestioned terror connections, getting nuclear weapons. What needs to be done about that? Foreign policy and national security will be front and center. The parties themselves are divided on Iraq, on Iran, on the question of democracy, on understanding what the threat is, and what kind of war it really is, and that introduces a huge element of unpredictability. It injects something new into the political landscape that we have lived with now for a couple of decades marked by a gradual, rolling Republican realignment.

So if my first point, the rolling realignment, and even my second point, the stability of the last decade, suggest stability and predictability, I very much want to emphasize that 9-11 and its effects suggest unpredictability and change. Change will continue. It's a big mistake to think, we've had the shock of 9-11, we've had the war in Afghanistan, and we've had the war in Iraq, and now all that is going to fade away, and we'll be back to usual. It's just not going to happen. The world is not going to permit that. There is not going to be a stable (albeit dangerous) cold-war type situation, in my judgment, in the foreseeable future. Neither will there be a 1990s type era where we can avoid really difficult choices and unpleasant entanglements in the world such as the ones in which we're now involved. We can't just have bombing campaigns from 30,000 feet. The world will not permit that, I don't think. And the debates about how to deal with this new world will be front and center. So the volatility introduced by 9-11 strikes me as trumping the predictability of the rolling realignment and the stability of the last decade.

Final observation—and it's a narrower point—is that 2008 will be the first presidential election in fifty-six years with neither an incumbent President running for reelection, nor an incumbent Vice President seeking to move up. Lately we've had Bush or Clinton running for reelection, or Gore running to succeed Clinton, and that introduces a certain, again, predictability to these races. An incumbent defends the administration of which he's a part. If the country is in good shape, the incumbent party wins, if the country is in bad shape, the incumbent loses. If the country is in ambiguous shape, as in 2004, you get a pretty close presidential election. There is a certain pattern to it.

But there is no incumbent in 2008, for the first time since 1952. You can even argue that the upcoming presidential is much more wild and unpredictable than '52, where it looked like Truman was going to run until the very end. Here we know Bush isn't going to run, unless he stages a coup. Bush isn't going to stage a coup, I don't think. It disappoints some people on some campuses when I say that. And Cheney's not going to run, I guess. I was speaking to a very liberal, kind of elderly, audience in New York about a month ago, and I couldn't resist saying, "You know, he might reconsider, and I hear there were rumors that the Cheney people were thinking about a candidacy," and a nice woman on the front row keeled over, and they had to call in the EMT people, so I felt bad about that, and I won't make that joke anymore. So no Bush, no Cheney, no incumbent—a wide open Republican race.

This is really unusual. Republicans tend to be somewhat hierarchical and predictable. Here's an amazing fact: On every Republican ticket since 1952, except the Goldwater saga in '64, since the year I was born, there has been a Nixon, a Dole, or a Bush on the Republican ticket. What a boring Party. So no Nixon, no Dole, no Bush. No single establishment candidate. No Bush-type, whom the whole money and business establishment rallies to, no single conservative movement candidate. No Reagan type, who rallies pretty much the entire conservative community. So we're facing the prospect of an extremely unpredictable Republican race with the two front runners, McCain and Giuliani, having problems with the Republican primary electorate. A couple of governors are going to run—Romney and Huckabee. Senators Frist, Allen, and Brownback and Newt Gingrich will run and will be, in my opinion, more formidable than people think. Who knows how that will turn out.

And then on the Democratic side, I expect a more wide open race than most people in Washington think. That is, I think Hillary is not a prohibitive favorite to be the nominee, but that is, of course, a question. Who knows? The Republican race will be interesting, and the Democratic race could really be fantastic. Kerry and Edwards both want to run. Each feels ill-used by the other from 2004. I think Edwards thinks that Kerry sent him off to secure states and didn't use him enough and take advantage of his popularity. Kerry thinks Edwards didn't fulfill the vice presidential role of sacrificing himself by being an attack dog. So they have some slight psychological issues. It will be good to see them on the stage together.

Of course, that will be nothing if Al Gore decides to run, which I certainly hope he will, along with Kerry. If Al Gore decides to run and he and Hillary Clinton can have their psychodrama—just think of the Democratic debates. You could easily have Hillary Clinton, Al Gore, John Kerry, John Edwards, Joe Biden (talking forever—that will be good), two or three governors—Vilsack, Richardson—and maybe another senator. Feingold, of course, will run as the antiwar candidate, except Gore will have stepped in to try to replace him as the antiwar candidate, so Feingold will be annoyed about that. And Al Sharpton, too—they will be excellent, these Democratic debates. Bill Clinton, sitting in the front row, looking up adoringly at Hillary. It will be fantastic.

Think about it. We really haven't ever seen as unpredictable a situation, where both parties have many plausible major candidates, and with the country at war, presumably, which introduces its own dynamic. The last two times we've had an election with troops really fighting in the field would be '68 and '52. In both of those years, the out-party won, so that could cheer Democrats up. It's also true that in both of those cases the more hawkish candidate won. I don't know that it's actually quite so good for Democrats to have a wartime election. If they seem to be the party that's not willing to prosecute the war, I very much agree with Hugh Hewitt.

For all these reasons, 2008 is likely to be a very volatile election, with a lot of candidates working in an entrepreneurial way—since none of them is an incumbent who must defend the past, and no one from the Bush administration is running—looking for issues to exploit. Immigration will certainly come into play, at least in the Republican primary, and I share Hugh's concerns about the way in which it does. But there will be all kinds of other issues—the war, obviously, on the Democratic side, but also issues we haven't even thought of—in terms of which the candidates will try to define themselves and make their name. So a bunch of entrepreneurial candidates running in two pretty wide open races, all in a post-9-11 context: It strikes me as a formula for considerable volatility and utter unpredictability, which I think will be fun. Thanks.

Question: On immigration, how do Republicans take a strong stand without alienating Hispanic voters?

Barone: California has been a testing ground for this. In '94 you had Proposition 187. I think what really hurt the Republicans on that was the implication that viewers drew from the ads run by Pete Wilson and some of those on behalf of 187, that all these immigrants were coming over for was welfare. Part of the reason that conclusion was drawn was because 187 was about welfare and government benefits. I think the Republican Party suffers from that. When you show contempt for people who work hard by saying they're just interested in welfare, they tend to vote against you.

At the same time, the Democrats, obviously, lost something with this driver's license bill for illegal aliens in the 2003 California election. So there is some down side risk for them on that side. I think there is down side risk for those of us, including me, who would like to see some kind of legalization and possibly a guest worker program, in addition to border security things. You see these demonstrations with the Mexican flags in downtown L.A., the proclamations of the Republic of Aztlan, and that we have lived here forever, which of course, in the case of the ancestors of almost all of these people is simply not correct. This area was essentially unoccupied, except by people of Apache and other descent before the treaty of Guadalupe Hidalgo, but I'm not exactly sure how this is going to play out. We've evidently had a collapse in the negotiations in the Senate towards an immigration bill today. Republicans will say Democrats blocked a border bill/security bill. If none is passed by this Congress, Democrats will say Republicans are incompetent at getting anything done on a pressing issue, and we'll see how much credence those charges have with voters.

Busch: I would just add to that. I think the whole question of voting rights brings up a broader issue. One way for Republicans to think about this issue is for them to not become nativists, but at the same time, insist on American citizenship and assimilation, which is a value that used to be taken for granted but has gone by the wayside due to some of the different manifestations of multiculturalism. But I think the answer that Republicans could give is that we welcome people to our country who want to become citizens, who want to vote, but you don't get to do that just by coming. You have to go through a process—you know, take the citizenship test, for goodness sakes. I think, frankly, the Republicans could make some hay, insisting on more civic education across the board, not just for immigrants, because I think that's an area where this country is really falling down, and it's paying a price, and it's going to pay a bigger price in the future.

Kristol: I'm all for civic education, but having been involved with this a bit when I was at the Education Department, the truth is, for my kids who went to public schools, you know, the civic education courses were the worst courses, because of course, they were just taught by leftwing political types who found that interesting, and I, myself, would have been happy to have them just take English, history, math, and science. One has to really concretely think through what is being proposed. I think Bush should take a look at the Education Department's funding of bilingual education, and make sure it's funding only ESL or immersion or bilingual programs that really make sure the kids learn English, which is, of course, for the sake of the kids, as much as anything else. It doesn't do that much good to get out not being fluent in English. There are things like that in a very concrete way that Republicans and Congress who are screaming and yelling about hordes coming over the border could do better if they are on the Education Committees to have some oversight over what the federal Education Department is doing, and I would say the same at the state level, because that is the most concrete thing. I don't take seriously the Mexican flags and all of that nonsense. The serious thing is, are the kids learning English and learning American history, or not. And that's a practical question. Most of these kids are in public schools. These public schools are controlled by legislatures, all of which have Republican members, and many of which have Republican majorities, and they should spend more time practically dealing with that question than complaining, I think, about the immigration problem.

Hewitt: I want to add one thought about the assimilation issue. I think the most important book in 2005 was Robert Kaplan's *Imperial Grunts*, where he spends three years in the company of the American military in places as far flung as Mongolia, Djibouti, Afghanistan, Iraq, Venezuela, and you'll be amazed at the number of Latinos who are on the front line of American's military right now. So the ultimate assimilation, of course, is to put on the uniform. And I believe it is true that while African-Americans are about represented where they are in the population, there is a huge number of Latino Americans who have seen in the military a path of progress and education, which is really the ultimate assimilation. And when you finish reading this book you say we really don't have an assimilation problem throughout most of that new culture. What we have is a lot of people who are uneasy with that new culture, and they're the ones that are having problems assimilating to the new America. It's really not about the willingness to be part of the American effort or exceptionalism. It's really about a reluctance to see their suburbia change as dramatically as it is changing, for example, in my home county of Orange.

Question: I have a two part question. First, are you arguing that Republicans are the only people who believe in American exceptionalism? And, how will Iraq affect the elections if things in Iraq do not improve?

Barone: Well, I didn't say Republicans had a monopoly on American exceptionalism. In fact, the numbers I cited show that the Democratic Party, if anything, is split a little more towards the American exceptionalism side than to what I would call, using Professor Samuel Huntington's word, the trans-national side. The trans-nationals like to denigrate people who believe in American exceptionalism as saying our country, right or wrong. Their view is this country is no better than any other country, and in effect, it's a whole lot worse in a whole lot of ways—we're really the evil cancer of human history, blah, blah, blah. You know, you get that on most university campuses. You can stuff yourself up to your eyeballs in that kind of garbage. I do think some Democrats are believers in, practitioners of, and good expounders of American exceptionalism. Bill Clinton was. You can find plenty in Bill Clinton's statements along those lines, and obviously, he was responding to something real in the electorate, among other things, so you do find that, but you find a large number that are the other way. I mean, Peter Beinart's new book, as I understand it, talks about the 1940s, when Democrats had a problem in that way, too. There was a Communist segment in the Democratic Party. The Communist Party endorsed Franklin Roosevelt in 1944. We were an ally of the Soviet Union then. Henry Wallace, Vice President and Secretary of Commerce under Truman, believed that the British Empire was a bigger adversary of the United States than the Soviet Union. He differed, totally, with Truman on this. You had important people in the labor movement— the Secretary/Treasurer of the CIO (Congress of Industrial Organizations), and so forth—who were part of the Henry Wallace line. And you had a group of liberal Democrats, of which some of the most famous are Eleanor Roosevelt, Hubert Humphrey, Walter Reuther and the United Auto Workers, who basically expelled these people from the Democratic Party, supported the United States, the Truman Administration policy in the Cold War, and stood up and created important institutions which helped stop the spread of totalitarianism, institutions that American conservatives at that time were very ill fixed to create, and American liberals did a great job.

I guess what Hugh is calling for is the Democrats who love this country, explain why do we have Michael Moore sitting next to President Carter at the Democratic National Convention? Why do we have half of the Democratic Senators going to Michael Moore's premier, Bill Nelson coming up, giving a big grin and a thumb's up, when Michael Moore, at the time of that premier, has on the front page of his website, the statement, "Americans are the stupidest people in the world?" I used to be a Democratic campaign consultant, but I never advised my clients to associate prominently with the person that said that Americans are the stupidest people in the world. It's sort of hard to win elections in this country without the votes of Americans (maybe in some parts of L.A. you can, but we'll leave that for a speech on the union). Why is Michael Moore there? Help me understand. I think the answer is that these people are so pickled in the juice of their hatred for George W. Bush that anybody who belittles or makes fun of George W. Bush is just fine with them, and I think that's shortsighted, politically.

Hewitt: I want to give you four examples which Democrats ought to have stood up in unison and condemned.

The first is that Abu Ghraib is a crime, not at all representative of the American military. In fact, I believe the Democratic Party seized upon it as an opportunity to score points against Bush, but gave off the impression that they thought it was representative of the American military, and not an aberration that was deeply, deeply repulsive to the men and women in uniform.

Two. When Richard Durbin took to the floor of the Senate and compared interrogation tactics at Gitmo [Guantanamo Bay] to those of Pol Pot, Stalin's thugs, Hitler's Nazis, it took him a week to back down, and the man who made him back down, interestingly enough, was a throwback to the old Democratic Party—it was the Mayor of Chicago, Richard Daley, whose son is in uniform. Daley called Durbin up and said, "You will apologize for this," and he did, tearfully, after standing tall. No one else called him on it, and even Major Daley did not do so publicly.

Three. When Joel Stein wrote in *The L.A. Times*, "I do not support the troops"—a very famous absurdity—again, Democrats did not take to the floor of the Senate to denounce him. They are put in a very, very difficult position whenever the excess of their party becomes representative of their party.

Four. And then, finally, *Daily Kos*. And this is the heart and soul of the Democratic Party. He is the most popular blogger, he is the most popular place on the web for Democrats to go to. And when American contractors were murdered and hung from lampposts in Fallujah, he, in essence, said, "Good." And Democrats did not step forward to demand an apology or to eject him from the party. In fact, he's the belle of the ball. I think the analogy is right to the problem that the Democratic Party had with Communists in 1948, they have anti-Americanism in a deep way poisoning their well. And unless and until they get rid of it, it's pretty hard to argue with Russ Feingold, when Russ Feingold says that the President is a criminal. On that note, thank you very much.

Barone: Well, as George W. Bush said in 2004, we're going to have an election about that, among other things. You know, we'll see. I mean, there's clearly a difference in response to Bush in the period of September 11 through early 2003, but after 2003, I think we're seeing a return to the sort of feelings that you had about Bush, and you get things like this. I'm told that one blogger said that he was present at the Center for American Progress—John Podesta's group. John Podesta is a very intelligent person who was Chief of Staff to Bill Clinton—a very serious person. They had Bush's State of the Union on television, and he said every time Bush talked about freedom or democracy, there was raucous laughter—Democrats showing contempt and laughter for an American President urging freedom and democracy in the world. I don't think that's a good thing for a political party.

Kristol: On the substance of Iraq, which I guess is what you were asking about, obviously, we've got to win in Iraq, and if it continues to be very tough, or even some sort of stalemate or worse, it could be like Truman with Korea, where he ended up with 25 percent popularity and Eisenhower was able to win. Whether the Democrats have an Eisenhower in 2008 is a question, but you can obviously be punished at the polls for either making the wrong decision or not carrying it out confidently.

Now it's tough, and obviously, Bush has been hurt badly by, I think, not going to war, but the failure to win the war and the failure for it to go as well as one would have hoped it would go. I think Iran will be a bigger issue, if you want a sort of perverse prediction. People vote prospectfully, not retrospectively, mostly. There will be no Bush Administration person running in 2008. I don't know how much Giuliani, McCain, Romney, or even Allen gets punished because of Secretary of Defense Rumsfeld during the Bush Administration. I think, therefore, 2008 will be a funny election, because people will be voting on which of these candidates can handle the world as it appears in November 2008. So I think something like Iran ends up perhaps being a more fundamental issue, and the general question of how to conduct this war and how to understand this war, than Iraq. I suppose if Iraq is totally disastrous, people might repudiate intervention, and the Democrats will win on a sort of anti-interventionist platform, I guess. No American presidential candidate—including '92, '96, and 2000, which were the years of the holiday from history—has won running as an anti-interventionist in the modern era since the beginning of World War II, or even since the run-up to World War II. Basically, when it comes to a presidential election or an off-year election, especially when you're at war or prospectively at war, dealing with Islamofacists who would like to kill a lot of Americans, people would prefer to err on the side of a strong Commander in Chief, rather than one who is reluctant to use U.S. force or thinks that the U.N. will deal with all of these problems. So I still think national security remains a huge problem for Democrats. And even in 2006, here's the question you have to ask yourself when people say Iraq is the greatest burden Bush faces, will Republicans do better or worse in 2006, if 2006 turns out to be a foreign policy and national security mid-term election. I think Republicans will probably do better.

Question: Will voters blame Republicans for economic troubles like huge deficits, stagnating wages, and a growing gap between the rich and everybody else?

Kristol: Some will think that and others will think everyone told us with the bursting of the dotcom bubble and the terror attack on 9-11 that we were going to have terrible economic times, and we've had 4 percent economic growth, 4.7 percent unemployment, and the market is back up to where it was before September 11, which is a petty impressive economic performance and maybe running those deficits was worth it. Incidentally, Bush's tax cuts, especially the 2003 supply-side tax cuts, were vindicated. If you want to follow no tax cut, European-style economic policies, take a look at Europe's economic performance, take a look at the U.S. economic performance. We had a perfectly good test case. Europe and the U.S. had comparable economic performances in the '90s. They actually had somewhat comparable economic policies in the '90s. We deviated radically when Bush became President. Bush cut taxes. No European country has pursued a supply-side tax cutting policy. Let's compare economic performance. I think Republicans have a pretty good argument on taxes and on economic growth in general.

Question: How many seats can Democrats pick up in the House elections?

Kristol: Let me give a footnote, and then Michael can give the long answer. There were two different studies just done recently that are pretty interesting. If you look through a national model of the current congressional generic poll, it is good for Democrats, you know, plus eight or something like that. I mean, even assume it slides back a little towards the norm, the Democrats end up with plus 6, plus 8 percent nationally, right now. They're plus 10 in most polls. By traditional standards, Democrats should win thirty-five seats or so in 2006, which would, of course, give them a comfortable majority.

If you do a district-by-district analysis and take into account gerrymandering and the shrinkage of competitive districts, Democrats only pick up eight seats, so a lot depends on what you think. Has the gerrymandering been so serious and has the decline of competitive race been so dramatic that history has changed? It might have, and even a big wind at the Democrats' back only gives them eight seats. My gut instinct, and this is not provable, is that the Republicans who are reassuring themselves that there are so many safe seats are whistling past the graveyard. If you get a big enough move and a small enough conservative and Republican turnout, and an energized Democratic base, a lot of seats that look safe, a lot of seats that were 59–41 or even 62–38 in 2004, where there wasn't a serious Democratic challenger, come back into play. In an off year the turnout goes down, and a lot depends, therefore, on who comes to the polls, and on good financing for a serious Democratic challenger. So my gut on this is that the Democrats can overcome, if they have a good general advantage. I don't think Republicans can be saved by gerrymandering.

Barone: Well, I've followed the House elections fairly closely, I guess, for I don't know, forty years, forty-four years. Generally I've found the district-by-district analysis tells you more than the political science formulas, which tended to be based more on periods of the 1930s and '40s, when you had a lot of straight ticket voting, when you didn't have media or candidate organizations getting the candidate's name out. You start to see differences in the 1950s. The district stuff makes the difference. That said, I wouldn't disagree very much with the analysis Bill has just given.

Sometimes when you have a major shift of opinion toward one party and away from the other, incumbents are caught napping and in seats that they seem to hold fairly easily. As far as the gerrymandering goes, one factor to keep in mind is that from '96 to '04 the numbers stayed very solid. I mean, the Republicans' percentage of popular vote for the House in those five elections was between 49 percent and 51 percent. The Democrats' percentage of the popular vote was between 46 percent and 48.5 percent. Those are very narrow and just slightly non-overlapping bands. Moreover, very little change in the contours of support.

In the early '90s coastal California moves towards the Democrats. Interior California moves towards the Republicans. Seats that have formerly been safe become marginal or safe for the other party. When that happens, gerrymanderers are frustrated in their purposes. Their handy-work becomes undone by the voters. That hasn't happened yet in this redistricting cycle. The redistricting following the 2000 census when Michael Berman did his masterpiece here in California was based on 2000 election results being the latest results. Those districts are still safe, because people aren't voting much different from how they voted in 2000.

If they start voting differently, some of those seats that are safe now might not be in the future, provided there is a serious candidate. I mean, dog candidates—the guy who fails to file a report with the FEC (Federal Election Commission) and spends $109 on his campaign—almost never get elected. It just doesn't happen and has not happened for thirty years. The closest you get was a couple of odd ducks that were swept in with the Republicans in '94, like Steve Stockman against Jack Brooks, the Chairman of the House Judiciary Committee. But you don't get the absolute dogs. You've got to have a candidate spending at least some hundreds of thousands of dollars, having some kind of a respectable claim on the office in order to pick off an incumbent, but you can sometimes pick off an incumbent. I'm not so worried.

I don't know how you reform redistricting. You can give it to a nonpartisan committee, but they sometimes end up having partisan rules. Texas was redistricted in '03 by Tom DeLay to put in place a Republican gerrymander to replace a Democratic gerrymander, which had been put in place in the 1990s by Martin Frost, and then when the legislature was unable to agree in '01, the Federal Court came in and said it would adapt the current plan because it's important that Texan incumbents have districts where they can win, because Texans get value out of having incumbents in Congress. Well, how do you get that out of the equal population standard? That's supposed to be equal protection of the voter. It seems to me it's a decision voters ought to make to keep incumbents in office for years because it's good for their state, or to kick them all out. It's up to the voters. In any case, you can have some of these nonpartisan panels, I suppose, though their plans will turn out to have partisan affects.

My own view is that given tight application of the equal population standard, it is very difficult for one party to entirely freeze the other out in any kind of competitive state over that ten-year inter-census period. Usually things change enough for the work of the gerrymanderers to become somewhat undone during that ten-year period. This decade that hasn't happened yet.

Notes

1. See Fred Barnes, *Rebel in Chief: Inside the Bold and Controversial Presidency of George W. Bush* (New York: Crown, 2006); Bruce Bartlett, *Impostor: How George W. Bush Bankrupted America and Betrayed the Reagan Legacy* (New York: Doubleday, 2006).

2. Peggy Noonan, "The Steamroller: The road to big government reaches a dead end at Jack Abramoff," *Wall Street Journal/Opinion Journal*, Thursday, January 5, 2006.

3. Ronald W. Reagan, *An American Life: The Autobiography* (New York: Simon & Schuster, 1990), p. 171.

Bibliography

Barnes, Fred. *Rebel in Chief: Inside the Bold and Controversial Presidency of George W. Bush*. New York: Crown, 2006.

Bartlett, Bruce. *Impostor: How George W. Bush Bankrupted America and Betrayed the Reagan Legacy*. New York: Doubleday, 2006.

Noonan, Peggy. "The Steamroller: The road to big government reaches a dead end at Jack Abramoff." *Wall Street Journal/Opinion Journal*, January 5, 2006.

Reagan, Ronald W. *An American Life: The Autobiography*. New York: Simon & Schuster, 1990.

Chapter Four

The Parties and Campaign Finance

Michael J. Malbin

The title of our panel invites broad discussion. In a bid to keep within manageable bounds, I shall focus on the Bipartisan Campaign Reform Act of 2002 (BCRA). To simplify further, the paper is organized around two main themes: party receipts and expenditures. After these topics, I shall briefly consider whether the changes we saw in the first election after BCRA are likely to be transient or long lasting. We end by asking whether these changes are good or bad for parties and for the political system.

Political Party Receipts after BCRA

The Bipartisan Campaign Reform Act of 2002 (otherwise known as the McCain–Feingold law) is well known for having prohibited national parties from raising "soft money." Beginning with the election of 2004, national political party committees would have to raise all of their funds in amounts and from sources that adhered to federal contribution limits. In addition, the law said that state parties would have use federal hard money, held in separate bank accounts, to pay for anything the law defined as 'federal election activity,' including some voter registration and getting out the vote.

Going into the 2004 elections, many scholars—including this one—made one or more of the following assumptions about what would likely happen. First, because half of the national parties' receipts in 2001–2002 came from soft money, they assumed the parties would have to cut back in 2004. Second, because 60 percent of the Democrats' money was soft money, compared to only 40 percent of the Republicans', they assumed the law would hurt Democrats more than Republicans, at least for the short term. Finally, because many state parties received a lot of money from the national parties, they assumed that BCRA would hurt the state parties too. I shall address these assumptions. To give credit where due, the material is based in part on work by others that appeared in a just published Campaign Finance Institute book I edited called *The Election After Reform*.

With respect to the first assumption: I suspect it is well known to people attending this conference that the national political parties raised record amounts in 2003–2004. As Anthony Corrado showed in his contribution to our book, the parties raised more in hard money alone than they did in hard and soft money combined in any previous year since disclosure (Corrado 2006). The basic numbers for the six national committees appear in Table 4.1.

Table 4.1. National Party Committee Fundraising, 1999–2004 (*$ millions*)

Committee	1999–2000			2001–2002			2003–2004	
	Hard	Soft	Total	Hard	Soft	Total	Hard	Total[a]
DNC	124.0	136.6	260.6	67.5	94.6	162.1	394.4	394.4
DSCC	40.5	63.7	104.2	48.4	95.1	143.5	88.7	88.7
DCCC	48.4	56.7	105.1	46.4	56.4	102.8	93.2	93.2
Democrats	212.9	245.2	458.1	162.3	246.1	408.4	576.2	576.2
RNC	212.8	166.2	379.0	170.1	113.9	284.0	392.4	392.4
NRSC	51.5	44.7	96.1	59.2	66.4	125.6	79.0	79.0
NRCC	97.3	47.3	144.6	123.6	69.7	193.3	185.7	185.7
Republicans	361.6	249.9	611.5	352.9	250.0	602.9	657.1	657.1
Total	574.5	495.1	1,069.6	515.2	496.1	1,011.3	1,233.2	1,233.2

Source: Anthony Corrado, "Party Finance in the Wake of BCRA: An Overview," in Michael J. Malbin (ed.), *The Election After Reform: Money, Politics and the Bipartisan Campaign Reform Act* (Lanham, MD: Rowman & Littlefield, 2006), p. 26. Derived from Federal Election Commission data. Totals are adjusted for transfers among committees, particularly in soft money accounts, and thus may vary slightly from the sums reported individually by committees.

[a] The 2004 Democratic totals include $29.6 million in excess primary funds transferred from the Kerry for President committee ($23.6 million to the DNC, $3 million to the DCCC). The Republican totals include $26 million in excess primary funds transferred from the Bush–Cheney '04 presidential committee ($24 million to the RNC, $1 million to the NRCC).

While the national parties *as a whole* raised much more in 2004 than in 2002, the committees did not all do equally well. All six committees raised much more *hard* money in 2004 than 2002, but none of the four congressional campaign committees fully made up for the *soft* money they had lost. The biggest surge came for the two national committees, which you would expect to be more important during a presidential election year. The surge was particularly impressive among Democrats. For the first time since post-Watergate disclosure, the Democratic National Committee (DNC) raised more than the Republican National Committee (RNC). In fact, the DNC raised nearly 50 percent more in 2004 in hard money alone than it did in hard and soft money combined in 2000. At the same time, the RNC just managed to make up for the loss of its soft money.

In 2005 the wealth seems to be spread more broadly. This time almost all of the party committees seem to be holding their own, not just the two national committees.

Table 4.2. Party Fundraising in Odd-Number Years, 1999–2005 *($ millions)*

	1999	2001	2003	2005
Republicans				
RNC				
Hard	44.0	67.3	107.8	105.4
Soft	29.2	48.1	**	**
Total	73.2	115.4	107.8	105.4
NRCC				
Hard	34.9	41.6	72.6	65.0
Soft	17.5	28.2	**	**
Total	52.4	69.8	72.6	65.0
NRSC				
Hard	16.4	25.0	26.4	35.5
Soft	13.5	23.8	**	**
Total	29.9	48.8	26.4	35.5
Combined Republican				
Hard	95.3	133.9	206.8	205.9
Soft	60.2	100.1	**	**
Total	155.5	234.0	206.8	205.9
Democrats				
DNC				
Hard	26.4	28.5	43.7	56.1
Soft	23.1	29.8	**	**
Total	49.5	58.3	43.7	56.1
DCCC				
Hard	15.2	16.7	26.6	42.9
Soft	18.4	18.1	**	**
Total	33.6	34.8	26.6	42.9
DSCC				
Hard	13.9	14.5	22.8	43.6
Soft	13.0	20.7	**	**
Total	26.9	35.2	22.8	43.6
Combined Democratic				
Hard	55.5	59.7	93.1	142.6
Soft	54.5	68.6	**	**
Total	110.0	128.3	93.1	142.6
Combined Two-Party Total				
Hard	150.8	193.6	299.9	348.5
Soft	114.7	168.7	**	**
Total	265.5	362.3	299.9	348.5

Source: Federal Election Commission

Five of the six party committees raised about as much hard money in 2005 as previous off-year hard and soft money combined. The Democratic Congressional and Senatorial Campaign Committees are actually well ahead of the old pace. The lagging committee this year, as two years ago, is the National Republican Senatorial Committee, but the problem (judging from the other Republican committees) does not stem from a shortage of GOP hard money donors in the system. And even this lagging committee has raised almost half again as much hard money in 2005 as it had in its best off-year before BCRA.

The upsurge in hard money contributions has come proportionally from donors who have given in all amounts, up to $25,000. However, the 50 percent of party money that used to come from the $25,000+ soft money donor is no longer in the party fundraising picture.

In addition, the amount of money coming in contributions of $200 or less has been impressive. Without soft money, the leaders of both parties redoubled their small donor fundraising efforts, increasing direct mail and Internet fundraising to unprecedented levels. The Republicans nearly doubled their small contributions over the last presidential cycle and the Democrats nearly tripled theirs. For the first time in decades, Democrats were raising the same percentage of their money in small contributions as were Republicans. As a result of these hard money efforts the national parties, even without soft money, had all the resources in 2004 that they had ever had in the past.

Table 4.3. Contributions to National Party Committees of Less than $200, 1999–2004

	1999–2000		2001–2002		2003–2004	
	$ mil.	% of total*	$ mil.	% of total*	$ mil.	% of total*
Republicans						
RNC	91.1	24%	102.9	38%	157.1	40%
NRCC	34.7	24%	39.7	21%	49.8	27%
NRSC	19.3	20%	20.2	16%	30.0	38%
Combined	145.1	24%	162.8	27%	236.9	36%
Democrats						
DNC	59.5	23%	37.8	23%	165.8	42%
DCCC	9.9	9%	11.2	11%	25.1	27%
DSCC	8.4	8%	9.7	7%	21.2	24%
Combined	77.8	17%	58.7	14%	212.1	37%
Two-Party Total	222.9	21%	221.5	22%	449.0	36%

Source: Federal Election Commission
Note: Total Receipts = Hard + soft money in 2000 and 2002; Hard money only in 2004.

Perhaps surprisingly, this national party fundraising seems not to have come at the expense of the state parties. The state parties did receive a significant amount of soft money in 2000 and 2002, transferred from the national party committees. Much of this was used to pay for television advertising. There was reason to be concerned that without these transfers, the state parties would be in worse shape. But according to Raymond La Raja's chapter in *The Election After Reform*, the state parties raised and spent about the same amount of money reportable to the Federal Election Commission in 2004 as in 2000, minus the transfers. In itself, that is not so surprising. Perhaps more significant was that once you remove spending for broadcast advertising, almost all of which was used for the national parties' targeted federal election priorities, the Republican state parties in 2004 spent more on their grassroots and other activities than they had in 2000, and Democratic state parties spent about the same amount. In other words, the soft money spent on advertising essentially was 'pass-through' money. Its absence did not have a major effect on the remaining activity conducted by the state parties (including grassroots voter mobilization and administration) or on their financial health (La Raja 2006).

II. The Party in Congress

One reason the parties have raised so much is, quite simply, that the stakes are so high. With majority control in both chambers of Congress narrowly held, and Presidential contest dramatically competitive, participants have incentives to make maximum efforts not only for themselves, but for their teams. At stake is not only winning or losing their own elections, but control over the policy agenda. The difference between being a chairman and ranking minority member

Table 4.4. Contributions from Members' Campaign Committees to Party Campaign Committees, 1990–2004, Full Cycles *($ millions)*

Cycle	House			Senate			Total
	Dem	Rep	Total	Dem	Rep	Total	
2004	18.3	19.4	37.7	8.1	3.2	11.2	86.5
2002	12.1	13.9	26.0	1.6	1.9	3.5	55.5
2000	7.6	14.5	22.1	1.1	2.6	3.7	47.8
1998	2.8	7.1	9.9	0.9	1.2	2.1	21.9
1996	1.2	4.0	5.2	0.2	0.2	0.4	10.9
1994	0.5	1.0	1.5	0.2	0.0	0.2	3.2
1992	0.5	0.0	0.5	0.2	0.0	0.2	1.1
1990	0.3	0.0	0.3	0.1	0.0	0.1	0.7

Source: Compiled by the Campaign Finance Institute from Federal Election Commission data.

is more significant than it once was. Because of these high stakes (as is well known from political science literature about the "conditional party government") the Members are willing delegate more power to party leaders. The followers accept that the leaders expect them to contribute money to the party campaign committees, with the understanding that the campaign committees will invest the money in the races most likely to affect majority control. The followers even accept the idea that leaders will use these contributions as a basis for distributing committee chairmanships and other positions of power inside the institution.

As the Table 4.4 shows, the phenomenon of members contributing to their parties' campaign committees has grown markedly in recent years. Contributions from Members to these committees began climbing in the mid-1990s, with House Republicans beginning in 1994, followed by House Democrats in 1996 and both Senate committees more recently (Bedlington and Malbin 2003).

Table 4.5. Contributions from Members' Campaign Committees to Party Campaign Committees, 2001–2005, Off-Years Only *($ millions)*

Cycle	House			Senate			Total
	Dem	Rep	Total	Dem	Rep	Total	
2005	8.1	3.8	11.8	2.0	.6	2.6	14.5
2003	5.8	1.5	7.3	.6	.2	.8	8.1
2001	3.3	1.0	4.3	0.0	* 0.0	0.0	4.3

Source: Complied by the Campaign Finance Institute from Federal Election Commission data.
Note: In 2001 Senate Democrats gave $10,000 and Senate Republicans gave $1,321.

If off-year numbers are a fair indication, this slope will continue heading upward in the coming midterm elections. House members gave 70 percent more to their party committees in 2003 than in 2001, and 63 percent more in 2005 than 2003. Senators, starting from a much lower base, showed an even steeper climb. Senators gave seventy-one *times* as much to their parties in 2003 as in 2001 and another four times as much in 2005 as in 2003.

BCRA is partially responsible for the level of money transferred. The 2002 law increased the amount an individual could give to a federal candidate from $1,000 (which was not indexed for inflation) to $2,000 indexed (worth $2,100 in 2006). Safe members have used the higher contribution limits to extract more money from individual supporters, especially lobbyists, and then have turned their excess funds over to the campaign committees. But the higher contribution limit does not come close to explaining the dollar amounts in these tables. Without the high stakes of chamber control, we would not have seen anything like this much of an increase.

III. Expenditures after *McConnell* v. *FEC*

The same conditional party government considerations that explain the increase in Member giving also go a long way toward explaining how the parties spend their money. The Federal Election Campaign Act of 1974 (FECA) placed clearly defined limits on the amount parties could give to candidates, or spend in a co-ordinated manner with them. For almost two decades after FECA this was how the parties supported their candidates. Because the parties typically raised more money than they could spend in the most hotly contested races, they used the extra money to support slightly less competitive non-incumbents, thus broadening the sphere of competition and helping to grow a farm team of candidates for the future. Studies, including one by this author, have shown that political party hard money under these conditions, in both federal and state elections, was the most pro-competitive, least pro-incumbent source of private funds in the system (Malbin and Gais 1998:145–52).

But the manner of political party spending changed with the growth of party soft money. Soft money was added to the federal law in 1979 for party building activities. Then Michael Dukakis (imitated by George H.W. Bush) saw in 1988 how to increase the use of soft money to help presidential candidates. This sky-rocketed with President Clinton's televised issue ads in 1995–1996. Under the soft money system, party spending limits effectively were removed. It therefore made strategic sense in a closely divided country for the parties to save their money for marginal states that could win the Electoral College, or the few House and Senate races that could determine control of the chamber. Virtually *none* of the soft money and none of the party funded issue advertising helped support or create competition because soft money and issue ads went to races in which two viable candidates were already competitive (Dwyre and Kolodny 2002).

However, soft money was not the only vehicle political parties legally have been able to use since 1996 to direct unlimited amounts of money toward specific races. In that year, the Supreme Court held (in *Colorado Republican Federal Campaign Committee et al.* v. *Federal Election Commission*, 518 U.S. 604 [1996]), that political parties had the same right to make independent expenditures as other organizations. The parties quickly began testing the waters. The National Republican Senatorial Committee in 1996 transferred $9.7 million to a separate staff that it in effect 'walled off' from the rest of the committee— putting it in a different location, using separate vendors, and not discussing advertising decisions with it. Democrats did not use the same tactics that year but did so later: the DCCC put about $2 million into independent spending in 2000 and another $1.3 million in 2002. For most years, however, most party committees let this tool lie unused, as soft money issue advertising became the unlimited spending of choice. The problems with independent spending, from the parties' perspective are, first, that the parties cannot coordinate with their own candidates (which they could do with issue ads) and, second, that independent spending can only be funded from hard money contributions raised under federal contribution limits. One reason hard money has that name is because it is harder money to raise.

BCRA's sponsors understood that banning soft money would lead the parties to move toward independent expenditures, which were constitutionally protected. However, the sponsors wanted to create a disincentive for using this form of spending, so they put a provision in the law that would have forced the parties to choose between independent and coordinated spending. During the debate some even said they expected the parties to go back to spreading their money around to more districts and states. The theory never was tested because this disincentive was one of the few provisions of BCRA that the Supreme Court overturned in *McConnell* v. *Federal Election Commission* (540 U.S. 93 [2003].)

Table 4.6 shows how the six national party committees in fact spent their money in 2003–2004. The Democratic National Committee put more than $120 million into independent spending, more than 90 percent of which was reported as negative advertising against President Bush. The RNC put less money into advertising but reportedly spent more than $100 million on voter mobilization—an activity that was done on the Democratic side more by the independent 527 committees. Independent spending was even more important proportionally for the four congressional committees. In a situation with no party spending limits,

Table 4.6. National Party Committee Expenditures in 2004 *($ millions)*

	a*	b	c	d	e	f
DNC	0.0ᵃ	16.1	120.9	18.6	155.1	889.9
DSCC	0.7	4.4	18.7	-	23.8	88.9
DCCC	0.4	2.4	36.9	-	39.7	92.4
Democrats	1.1	22.9	176.5	18.6	218.6	1071.2
RNC	0.2	16.1	18.3	45.8	80.4	882.6
NRSC	0.8	8.4	19.4	-	28.6	78.7
NRCC	0.5	3.2	47.3	-	51.0	184.8
Republicans	1.6	27.7	85.0	45.8	160.0	1046.1
Total	2.7	50.6	261.0	64.6	378.6	2117.3

Source: Federal Election Commission. Totals may not add due to rounding. Based on Anthony Corrado, 'Party Finance in the Wake of BCRA: An Overview,' in Michael J. Malbin (ed.), *The Election After Reform: Money, Politics and the Bipartisan Campaign Reform Act* (Lanham, MD: Rowman & Littlefield, 2006), p. 33.
*a = contributions; b = coordinated expenditures; c = independent expenditures; d = generic ads; e = total candidate support; f = total expenditures
ᵃ The DNC made only $7,000 in contributions to candidates.

few hotly contested races, and high stakes battle over narrow majority control, the parties chose to concentrate their resources heavily in a relatively few contests. According to Diane Dwyre and Robin Kolodny's contribution to *The Election After Reform*, $38 million in Senate party independent spending went to only twelve races, with the parties committing more than $1 million on each side in eight. In House races, the parties' $84 million focused on thirty races. If you do the math: that averages to more than $1 million per candidate in these House races as well. In seventeen cases, party spending came to more than what the candidates could raise and spend for themselves (Dwyre and Kolodny, 2006: 48–49).

Table 4.7. Party Commitment to Selected House Races: Independent and Coordinated Expenditures, as a Percent of Candidate Spending

	>100%	75–100%	50–75%	25–50%	Total
Democrats	7	3	8	8	26
Republicans	10	4	9	8	31
Total	17	7	17	16	57

Source: Compiled from FEC data. Originally appeared in Diana Dwyre and Robin Kolodny, 'The Parties' Congressional Campaign Committees in 2004,' in Michael J. Malbin (ed.), *The Election After Reform: Money, Politics and the Bipartisan Campaign Reform Act* (Lanham, MD: Rowman & Littlefield, 2006), p. 50.

The net effect, therefore, seems to be that BCRA had little effect on the way the parties spend their money. They focused their money in the way that made the most strategic sense for them. Independent spending (funded out of limited contributions) bought what soft money used to buy. Short of a constitutional amendment it is hard to see how this could be otherwise, or why it should be.

IV. Summary and Implications

So far this paper has argued that prohibiting soft money did no harm to party receipts in 2004 and did little to change the parties' spending patterns. I conclude with two further questions: First, is this likely to continue? Second, is it good for the system?

It is hard to be confident predicting future party fundraising without better information about the motives of those who participate now. There has not been a good survey of political party donors in recent years. As an admittedly imperfect substitute, I turn briefly to the results of intensive data analysis done by the Campaign Finance Institute of presidential campaign donors in 2004, as well as the results of a survey of 2004 presidential donors conducted by George Washington University's Institute for Politics Democracy and the Internet, in collaboration with CFI. The report on that survey was published in March and is available on either of the two organizations' websites (Graf, et al. 2006). The most important conclusions from these two efforts for today's subject were these:

- ❖ Many more people gave money to presidential candidates in 2004 (about 3 million donors) than in 2000 (when there about 800,000 contributed). Within these totals, the number of small donors who gave less than $200 appears to have quadrupled, from about 625,000 to somewhere between 2.1 and 2.8 million.
- ❖ We used to think of the donor pool as a small number of rich people who would keep giving year after year. We learned from CFI's analysis of all presidential donors that there is much more churning in and out in the system than we had ever suspected.

  - For example, we (like most political professionals) had expected that virtually all of George W. Bush's major donors in 2000 would repeat in 2004. It turns out that only 30 percent of them did.

  - Bush was not alone. Only 24 percent of Al Gore's 2000 donors and 21 percent of Bill Bradley's gave to *any* of the Democrats in 2004.

As a result of these and other analyses, we are beginning to get a new view of the pool of potential donors that is more unpredictable and that in some respects offers more opportunity for future campaigns than many political professionals used to think.

- ❖ Unsolicited donors and the Internet: About 40 percent of the online donors said they contributed *without* being asked. This compares to about one-quarter of the offline donors.
- ❖ Internet empowerment and civic engagement: The Internet is leveling the playing field between large donors and small donors. Being online makes it easier for small donors to connect with others, find information and be politically active.
- ❖ The Internet and young donors: Nearly all young donors gave online (more than 80 percent).
- ❖ Small donors' political views: Finally, there has been concern expressed that small donors may be more polarized or more extreme in their views than major donors. We found, contrary to conventional wisdom, that small donors were no more polarized or extreme in their views than people who gave large amounts of money. However, both sets were more polarized than the average voter, and both sets were likely to have given because of their intense feelings about the issues or candidates.

We take mixed information away from these findings as we try to predict future party fundraising. The intensity of feelings about the issues in 2004, as well as the intensity of feelings (pro and con) about President Bush, persuaded many new donors to participate. Without the same issues, and with the amount of in-and-out participation we found, we would ordinarily expect many of the 2004 first-timers not to come back. However, the ease of Internet communication, and its importance among young donors, leads us to expect, in the opposite direction, that many of these first timers will be receiving reinforcing messages that will engage them as Internet activists. They are more likely to remain engaged in the larger political process through these communications than a person to whom the next communication looks like the day's junk mail. In short, I expect the parties to keep at least some their new donors from this election to the next and also expect they will have both the motivation and capacity to continue to grow.

Our final question is whether the changes to political parties on the whole have been good or bad for the system. During the debate over BCRA some who were concerned about the law's potential effects said they feared that reducing parties' resources would weaken their ability to act as buffers between public officials and interest groups. I would argue first, that in a system of unlimited contributions the party leaders were acting more as facilitators than as buffers. And second, party resources clearly were not harmed.

Having refuted these arguments, it is important to acknowledge that public policy is probably nearing the edge of what can be accomplished profitably through a strategy of limits. Limits have been useful tools for attenuating the direct ties between public officials and major donors. I believe this is good. One may disagree with this evaluation after balancing the various effects of a contribution limit,[1] but even so one would have to acknowledge that these limits are relevant for attenuating this connection. However, it is not possible to argue that limits effectively do much to reach more affirmative goals. Limits are about preventing harm more than they are about accomplishing good. They cannot *build* the kind of democratic participation or party system one hopes to see.

Building requires reconnecting. It requires persuading parties and candidates to reach out. This year's growth in participation was encouraging and the Internet holds promise for the future, but the promise of a free wheeling Internet probably will not be enough. If the goal is to build a system in which citizens in fact participate, then public policy still has an important role to play. On the negative side, policy makers who support contribution limits, as I do, should keep in mind that even good policies can have harmful side effects. When writing regulations to enforce limits, it is important to be sensitive that attempting perfection may stifle participation.

In a more positive vein: participation by small donors is still far from what at least I would like to see. Public policy can be used to help improve this situation. The policies most directly aimed at this goal are political contribution tax credits or rebates on the one hand, and public financing systems on the other, particularly ones that use matching funds rather than flat grants.

The Campaign Finance Institute is publicly identified with a proposal to change the matching fund system for the presidential primaries. The current system gives participating candidates $1 in matching for each of the first $250 a candidate raises from individual contributors. We would change the current one-for-one match for the first $250 to a three-for-one match for the first $100. The goal, obviously, is to heighten the importance of small contributions. Seven-eighths of the presidential donors in 2000 gave less than $100, but donors who gave $1,000 or more gave the bulk of the money. Unfortunately, comparable data for the $100 donors are not available for 2004, but based on the material we do have to $200 donors, the thrust of the comparison is not likely to have changed.

You may ask whether there still is a problem with small donor participation. There is. Almost all of the small donors last time, except for Howard Dean's, came into the system after Super Tuesday. Until Super Tuesday, donors of $1,000 or more accounted for 70 percent of the other presidential candidates' fundraising. If you think it is important for small donors to participate while there is still a contest for them to engage, then it is important to address this through public policy.

Some people at this conference have stated publicly that the presidential system is as good as dead, and they are right if the system is not changed. But it would be truly a shame not to change it. The problem is not with the matching money *per se* but with the spending limit. In order to get any matching money under current law, a candidate has to agree to a spending limit that would be too low even if all of the candidates followed it, and absurdly unrealistic once one of the serious candidates decides to break free. The bulk of this paper has been about how campaign finance laws affect the parties. For a couple of paragraphs let us reverse the causal direction to think about how the parties' rules affect the candidates' ability to finance their speech. The Democratic Party is about to make the nomination system even more frontloaded than it was in 2004. Once one candidate opts out of public funding to go over the spending limit, it becomes nearly impossible for others to be heard unless they step outside the system too. But with the primary calendar so compressed, it becomes impossible for that person to get the needed money unless s/he is rich, or an establishment-backed front runner, or can catch the wave-of-the moment for Internet fundraising. The rest of the qualified candidates need not apply.

It was bad enough when most candidates' chances could be killed *by* the first one or two states. Soon they will not even be able to afford to be heard in the first states. Of course, the establishment front runner might well be a good candidate. But how can a party know that the candidate faces a serious test? The public is better off when it has a chance both to hear and be heard. What it soon will hear will be severely truncated, even more than in recent years, unless the public financing system is changed.

Fortunately, the solutions are simple. They involve modest, incremental changes to the spending limits. CFI recommends raising the spending limit for participating candidates in the primaries to the same level as the general election but removing the limit entirely if the candidates' opponent steps outside the system. In this situation, everyone will abide by the limit as long as the others do too. But if one should opt out, the underdog could still use public matching funds as a floor without have to commit spending limit suicide to do so.

The above discussion of public funding focused on candidates because parties are less likely than candidates to be helped significantly by any form of public funding—whether tax credits, matching funds or a grants. Some states do give tax credits for party contributions, but party contributors are more likely to be repeaters than first timers. First time donors are more likely to be brought into the system by candidates, especially presidential candidates. It is from presidential candidates that the parties will gain their future identities as well as their ongoing supporters. That is why the health of the presidential system implicates the health of the parties.

Having said this, I believe the blocks are in place for significant rebuilding. The 2004 growth in participation was important. The Internet is already proving itself and promising more. So far the Democrats have done a better job using the Internet for fundraising and the Republicans for organizing, but each is learning from the other. The passions of 2004 will abate but some of the gains in participation will linger—*if* they are nurtured properly by the parties, their candidates, and a supportive set of public policies.

Questions and Answers

Question: You mentioned that many scholars' predictions were wrong about McCain-Feingold, including some of yours. On which of your predictions were you wrong?

Michael Malbin: I predicted that the parties would raise less money but would recoup some of the soft money they lost. It turns out they did better than I and most others had expected. I don't think that was a huge error, but it was an error. The parties made better use of the Internet than we expected and the war heightened people's desire to give. Were we wrong because outside groups were stimulated and large donors stayed in the process? No. Many people expected that, although not to the extent that happened. I do think Senators McCain and Feingold thought that you could dampen the importance of major donors to the so-called of 527 political committees that were important in 2004 through contribution limits that relied not on the 2002 law but under provisions of the original 1974 law. But most people predicted that at least some of the major soft money donors would find other avenues. The main focus of the bill was about attenuating the relationship between office holder and donors, not about shutting down outside speech, and the outside speech did go up faster than we predicted.

Question: The Campaign Finance Institute issued a report a couple of months ago, saying that this could be a good year for the Democrats. Could you please tell us more about that?

Malbin: Yes. We issued a report in early February, based on congressional candidates' finances through the end of 2005. I need to reconstruct some of this, but we were looking to see how many non-incumbent candidates of each party had raised a significant amount of early money this year and in past election cycles. There are no hard and fast rules about how much is "enough" for the early stages. Candidates can still enter the race relatively late and do well, particularly in late primary states. But the number of states with late congressional primaries has been fairly constant from year to year. So we looked for general guidelines at how much typical candidates who ended up with at least 45 percent of the vote in past years had raised by this time in the cycle. We thought that if an unusual number of candidates had raised $50,000, $75,000 or $100,000 in the early stages this year, we should pay attention. Based on past experience, this seemed to be enough early money for the first stages of a serious startup. That's not enough for a full campaign. A challenger will need ten or twenty times that much at the end of the day. But startup money is the hardest money to raise. So we took $100,000 as an easy cutoff point, and reported that forty-one Republican incumbents were already facing Democratic challengers who had raised that much money, and almost no Democratic incumbents at that point were facing well funded Republican challengers. That is, potentially viable Democrats were choosing to get into the race and were raising money, but potentially viable Republican challengers were not showing up. As a result, we said that if the issues in the election produced a national tide, there were more than enough Republican seats with well funded Democratic challengers who would be in a position to take advantage of that tide and put control of the chamber at issue—many more than were being reported at that time of the year by the leading national pundits. In fact, I think we were the first, or among the first, to have been saying that control of the chamber was at stake in 2006. We'll do another of these reports in April, but I do not expect the fundamental picture to have changed.

Question: What about the increase in the individual contribution amount?

Malbin: The law increased the hard money contribution limit to $2,000. That increase was opposed by some of the reform groups. A number of us thought that was a good idea. Raising the limit to $2,000 made up about half of the value that contribution limits had lost through inflation over time. The increase in the hard money contribution limit to the parties was actually not the source of the most of the surge of party money, but it helped. There were people who gave $25,000 instead of $20,000, and that probably accounted for a part of the increase. I think what really helped was members of Congress raising money in $2,000 chunks and then giving their extra money to the party committees.

Question: What do you think about disclosure as an alternative or a complement to regulation in empowering small donors?

Malbin: I agree that empowering small donors is not a regulatory issue, but I do believe there are policies that can help strengthen candidates' incentives to try to look for small donors—for example, 100 percent small tax credits, rebates as in the State of Minnesota, a three-for-one public funding match, or four-for-one match, such as in New York City. This is not about using regulation to deter or prohibit certain behavior; it's about using money to reward behavior. Then, to prevent the costs of a matching fund from skyrocketing, you put a limit on the amount of such money that any one candidate can get. If it's a rebate or tax incentive, then the donors decide who gets the money. But you cap the amount of credit that any donor can take, and you can also put an income cap on those who take a credit so it does not just reward rich folks who already give.

On the disclosure side, there's a really small issue I want to mention because the Campaign Finance Institute is involved in it. I can't believe the Senate does not disclose its own campaign finance reports electronically. All other federal candidates and committees are required to do so. We've been lobbying that issue all year. A bill to require this has a fair number of cosponsors, but nobody bothers bringing the issue up for a vote. It's very interesting.

Let me turn now to interest group activities that are not now covered by disclosure. I think you can require disclosure of more organizations in more circumstances than you can reach through limits. Of course there are freedom costs to disclosure too, and so there are places where you may not want to go. But there's a lot you can do, both technically and legally, to expand the disclosure realm.

Notes

1. Some have expressed a concern that contribution limits make it hard for non-incumbents or minor parties to get started. This is a legitimate concern that could be addressed with a higher contribution limit for seed money. However, the issue is not relevant for contributions to the major parties.

Bibliography

Bedlington, Anne H., and Michael J. Malbin. "The Party as an Extended Network: Members Giving to Each Other and to their Parties." In *Life after Reform: When the Bipartisan Campaign Reform Act Meets Politics*. Edited by Michael J. Malbin, 121–137. Lanham, MD: Rowman & Littlefield, 2003.

Corrado, Anthony. "Party Finance in the Wake of BCRA: An Overview." In *The Election after Reform: Money, Politics and the Bipartisan Campaign Reform Act*. Edited by Michael J. Malbin, 19–37. Lanham, MD: Rowman & Littlefield, 2006.

Dwyre, Diana, and Robin Kolodny. "Throwing Out the Rule Book: Party Financing of the 2000 Election." In *Financing the 2000 Elections*. Edited by David B. Magleby. Washington, D.C.: The Brookings Institution, 2002.

———. "The Parties' Congressional Campaign Committees in 2004," In *The Election after Reform: Money, Politics and the Bipartisan Campaign Reform Act*. Edited by Michael J. Malbin, 38–56. Lanham, MD: Rowman & Littlefield, 2006.

Graf, Joseph, Grant Reeher, Michael J. Malbin and Costas Panagopoulos. *Small Donors and Online Giving: A Study of Donors to the 2004 Presidential Campaigns*. Washington, DC: George Washington University, Institute for Politics, Democracy and the Internet, 2006. Copies available electronically at www.ipdi.org and www.CampaignFinanceInstitute.org.

La Raja, Raymond J. "State and Local Political Parties." In *The Election after Reform: Money, Politics and the Bipartisan Campaign Reform Act*. Edited by Michael J. Malbin, 57–75. Lanham, MD: Rowman & Littlefield, 2006.

Malbin, Michael J. and Thomas L. Gais. *The Day after Reform: Sobering Campaign Finance Lessons from the American States.* Albany NY: Rockefeller Institute Press, 1998. Distributed by The Brookings Institution, Washington D.C.

Chapter Five

The Future of Party Organization

Nelson W. Polsby

I'd like to begin by thanking the organizers of this conference for assembling in one place so many old friends and colleagues, and other people from whom I've learned so much about political parties over the years. Occasions like this one occur less frequently than I would like under academic auspices where scholars and other serious students of American life can reflect on some of the fundamental trends and forces that animate our political institutions, free from the felt obligation to spin. I'm sure you all recognize the last couple of panels depart from that characterization. I'm going to propose a perspective on American political parties that will, I'm sure, strike most of you as unoriginal.

The idea of party, even party organization, is pretty broad and encompassing. It is more or less traditional to begin with V. O. Key's Holy Trinity, distinguishing among parties as they exist in the minds of citizens and voters, providing frames for political loyalties, attitudes, preferences and even ideologies; parties as they exist in America's legislatures to assist in producing or preventing policy outcomes; and parties as they organize in various constituencies to nominate and elect candidates for public office. I take my mandate today to talk mostly about the third sense of the term, some about the second, and as little as possible about the first. Even accepting these limitations, there is too much to talk about in one go, and so I will simply make a few points more or less on my topic, and hope that that will suffice to give some orientation to further discussion.

My point of departure will be a recommendation that we consider political parties as intermediary organizations managing relationships between political leaders and the rest of us. In the United States they are not the only political intermediary organizations, and so an evaluation of their future can best be conducted in light of trends in the society that may tend to substitute and interchange parties with plausible alternative organizational entities, such as interest groups, the news media, and now increasingly the Internet.

Interest groups, like parties, aggregate and express preferences of ordinary citizens for and against various public policies. Typically, parties accept a broader brief than any particular interest group. The virtue of parties as compared with interest groups is that they undertake to effect tradeoffs among citizen demands, and do not merely advocate for groups in the population. I suppose in principle, interest groups could spontaneously create grand coalitions through a series of bilateral treaties, thus solving the acute social problem, taking account of many interests in a context of a large, heterogeneous population existing within resource limitations, economic scarcities and time constraints.

But characteristically, interest groups do not do this, and I conjecture that in the absence of parties they would find it extremely difficult to reach broadly acceptable conclusions about priorities and strategies for achieving policy results. Hence, interest group leaders and members find it prudent to adopt allegiances that go beyond group loyalties and seek alliances with political parties in order to help themselves achieve their policy goals.

Mass media communicate priorities and preferences among large populations with great efficiency, thus identifying issues and possible solutions to social problems, as parties also do. While the news media disseminate this sort of information well, they listen far less efficiently than they broadcast, and far less efficiently than parties. Typically, the media are organizations in which the few set agendas for the many, and those few go through no regularized process that establishes their legitimacy to do so. There are craft norms, to be sure, but the American Constitution and legal traditions forbid the invocation of sanctions from outside the guild, except in rare circumstances. A climate of vigorous competition among news media organizations helps a little, but I think no competent observer would claim that the press, even broadly considered, is subjected to the accountability processes routinely applied to parties, party officials, and elected officials operating under partisan auspices.

A new and formidable challenge to the news media, to established interest groups, and to parties arises from the agenda-setting capabilities of Internet communication in which there is a decentralization of functions such that new interest groups not dependent upon geographic propinquity can form rapidly out of thin air, and topics of concern can be broached by anyone at all and can bypass editorial supervision that in principle might provide elementary reality checks. Thus, the cost of doing business this way can be the introduction of new level of slanderous, or at a minimum inaccurate, content to political discourse.

Parties have a capacity to filter and weed out some of this stuff, but when conditions of partisan competition take a certain shape, as we know, parties are more likely to try to exploit than to limit lies floated in the blogosphere.

Okay, in these sparse comments, I imagine we might detect a few clues to the future of party organizations. Although they still perform indispensable functions and have extremely valuable properties, that is, valuable for the proper operation of a democratic political system, they are, at several margins, vulnerable to being replaced and substituted for by institutional complexes with quite different properties and methods of doing business. We see this in nomination processes, in the raising and disposal of political issues, and political discourse more generally. It affects political careers and it affects the writing of history; hence, the stock of memories our polity holds in common.

The most famous, and I dare say, the most consequential such substitution in recent American history took place as a result of the reforms of the presidential nomination process of 1969–1970, in which state party organizations and their leaders were relegated to supporting roles and effectively substituted for by primary electorates, chiefly mobilized and instructed by the news media. While it may be true that the state parties have in some cases made strenuous efforts to adapt in order to regain influence in presidential nominations over the last thirty years, it has been rough sledding all the way, and as far as I can see they have not regained their former position. This is the best example I know illustrating the proposition that American political institutions do change, or at least have changes thrust upon them.

Another example might be the saga of the regulation of political money. In general it has been noticed that parties and interest groups adopt different patterns of investment in candidates for public office. Parties invest early, interest groups late, parties make an effort to help marginal candidates, and interest groups prefer sure things. Hence, regulations on money that tighten restrictions on party money are regularly predicted to send more money to campaigns through interest groups with, I assume, the indicated long-run effects on the basic conditions of democratic competition. Of course, this effect may be delayed if, in the course of shutting down party money, they double the limits on hard money that will, obviously, help parties at least over the short run maintain their position.

While I have the floor, there are a small number of other points I would like to make about American political parties that I have not recently seen mentioned. They may interest political scientists more than the people who are, however briefly, incarcerated in rooms like this one to listen, in which case I offer my apologies for running on.

The first on this subsidiary list is that while we frequently and rightly refer to American political parties as decentralized, we less often refer to them as ephemeral. This is meant to indicate that they are fragmented in time as well as in space. They arise and take their shapes in response to periodic elections, and then quite frequently disappear. The fact is, there isn't much careful, systematic work on which scholars can rely in making this point, but it seems to me that while it is possible to point to actual offices with filing cabinets and telephone numbers in Washington, D.C., and say, "There is the location of the Republican National Committee and the Democratic National Committee, and the respective party campaign committees of the House and the Senate," the situation at the state and local levels is highly variable and not susceptible to compact description. In some places, pretty clearly, the same organization supports candidates for local office, for the State Assembly, and for Congress, and in some places pretty clearly these various party tasks are done on a much more ad hoc basis. Party committees exist at the grassroots, but these roots are much better nourished in some places and for some parties than others.

I simply don't know what to say about the future of party organizations at this level, where I scarcely know what to say about their present. For anyone who is interested in getting a grip on the scope of the problem, simply take a look at the career lines of current members of the U.S. Senate or the House of Representatives, and ask how they arrived at the nomination that put them on the ticket, and what role leaders of regular party organizations played in the process as compared with labor unions, other interest group leaders, news media, party notables from outside the constituency, or what have you.

A long time ago I did a study of congressional recruitment in the state of Connecticut, in which I found that the Democrats and Republicans did it differently because the Democratic Party in the state was rooted in the party organizations of four major and ten or so minor cities, the leaders of which could easily keep an eye on one another and bargain, whereas the Republicans controlled most of the rest of the 169 towns and had to make use of the state legislative delegations to sort things out. Well, that was then, a half a century ago. Who knows what it is now? My point is simply that any persuasive argument about the future of parties will require a hard look at fifty different states and a minimum of two parties per state. This is the basis of my long held conviction that the United States does not have a two-party system as the textbooks say, but more like a hundred-party system. Moreover, an overview of the two-party labels that these hundred parties use, strongly suggest something beyond the stale news that Democrats and Republicans are not Tweedle Dum and Tweedle Dee in all but their location on a simple left, right ideological scale.

My late colleague, Herbert McClosky, sorted that out half a century ago by showing that it is party activists and not party rank and file who split definitively on public issues and party rank and file of both parties pile up in the middle most of the time. This conclusion has held up well over the years. We can, however, say something more. Organizationally, the two parties are different. Republicans are ideologically more united—sometimes a lot more united. They coordinate themselves through policy agreement. Democrats over the last half century have been the more heterogeneous party. They coordinate by bargaining. There is varied evidence for this conclusion. Most observers of delegates at national conventions of the two parties, I think, agree with Jo Freeman and Byron Shafer that Democrats at the conventions go to subgroup caucuses to make demands on their leaders. Republicans go to parties or go shopping, and await marching orders.

In my time the only persistent issues that divide Republicans at their annual conventions have to do with what constitutes true belief. Meanwhile, by reforming the nominating processes in 1969 and 1970, the Democrats eliminated opportunities for both parties to bargain internally and substituted reliance on plebiscitary processes, primary elections. This hurt the bargaining dependent Democrats much more than the ideologically coherent Republicans, and made it hard to mobilize the Democratic majority that, in fact, existed out in the general population. The result was a string of otherwise inexplicable Republican victories in presidential elections.

Bill Mayer and I once did a study that fortifies the point I've been trying to make. There is, as we all know, a simple statistical measure of central tendency, which tells an observer how closely respondents cluster around the middle of a distribution of responses. Well, using data from the national election studies conducted between 1968 and 1996, we found that Democratic respondents were more spread out than Republicans on 115 of 127 items measuring opinions on public policy issues. This may change in the future if the addition of Dixiecrats and churchgoing Catholics and Christian fundamentalists broaden the Republican Party, as some observers think may have happened. As far as I'm concerned the jury is still out on this proposition, since the principle that seems to be driving recruitment of the new bodies is ideological agreement. Maybe the subtraction of some of these groups from the Democratic coalition would provide the stronger effect, making the two parties more alike. But here again, to my knowledge, the definitive work is yet to be done.

I think I'll stop now. You've been very patient. I appreciate it. I hope these conjectures stir further and deeper thought on what I think we all agree is a most absorbing subject. Thank you.

Questions and Answers

Question: What will the effect of bloggers be on the parties and on politics in general?

Nelson Polsby: Well, we don't know yet. Obviously, they may have more impact on interest groups, actually, than on parties, simply because they can create interest groups, as I said, out of thin air. The other thing they can do is quite fascinating. They can put things on the agenda that nobody wants on the agenda, and for that they interact with the news media, because somebody like Matt Drudge, for example, can put out any kind of slander, and after a while *The New York Times* thinks it's all right to publish it, because after all, it's out there. It was the same principle you may recall (you don't recall—you're too young, you lucky person), when the news media regularly printed stuff they knew was nonsense from Joe McCarthy, because he said it, didn't he? So this is now a technologically souped-up system which, at its worst, can be like McCarthy, and at its best can surface hidden things which people don't know enough to talk about through their usual interest group or party channels.

Question: Is there any chance of the two-party monopoly weakening?

Polsby: Jesse Ventura in the state of Minnesota got to be governor running on the Reform Party ticket. One of the things that people don't realize—everybody in this room realizes it, but a lot of my students don't realize it—is that the word disenfranchisement is quite frequently used, and what they mean is they lost an election. They are unaware of the fact that in many states there are many alternatives for president on the ballot, and people are perfectly free to vote for them, and they don't. Now is that a disenfranchisement or is that simple calculation? More likely what it is is a lack of familiarity with anybody but the main players. In any event, it seems to me our system is very strongly skewed toward two major parties.

Question: How do we get away from that?

Polsby: Sure. There are at least two directions you can move. There are many one-party systems in the world, and if you prefer that, move to Bulgaria or wherever. And there are, of course, systems where there are three to five parties—Scandinavia and places like that. You might say the UK is a kind of a two-and-a-half party system, mainly. The Liberal Democrats generally get more votes than they get a percentage of seats in parliament. The Lib Dems are a wonderful, mellow group of people, mostly from the Scottish borders and the west country and places where there are a lot of sheep, and people who tend to wear sandals. And they just fired their leader. They take these things seriously. They decided Charles Kennedy drank too much and so they got rid of him, which led to the remark that somebody said, "What does Charles Kennedy have in common with Julius Caesar? Both were done in by men wearing sandals."

Question: How do you feel about the different ways states treat third-party fusion?

Polsby: How do I feel about fusion where it's illegal in some states and legal in others? I don't have any feelings about it at all. I am interested in the phenomenon. I think, for example, in the state of New York, for a very, very long time, fusion was a sensible way of aggregating interest groups that were mostly, obviously, affiliated with the Democratic Party. The Liberal party of New York was dominated by the garment workers for a long time. You, of course, are familiar with the wonderful story that Dr. Sherwin Nuland tells about preparing his aged aunt for a naturalization exam, and he said she was absolutely terrific—a very bright woman. One of the questions—it was an enormous list in those days—it was a long time ago now. But she knew who the president of the Confederacy was—Jefferson Davis. And the president of the union—David Dubinsky. So that was fusion.

Then, on the other hand, fusion in other places, for example, in Minnesota in the 1940s, had a tendency to fragment liberal sentiment in such a way that Republicans elected a whole bunch of people they probably shouldn't have elected, and Hubert Humphrey, the vastly under-rated Hubert Humphrey, got in there and put the Farmer Labor party together with the Democratic Party and made them a much more formidable political force than had been true when they were all split up. So, of course, a separate issue is, should it be made illegal? My gut feeling about anything like that is if you can avoid compulsion, you are probably better off.

Question: How many countries use the U.S. system of democracy, and what might be some alternatives?

Polsby: I don't know the quantitative stuff. Bob Dahl's most recent book, written at age eighty-nine about various deficiencies of the U.S. Constitution, I think citing work mostly by Juan Linz and some others, points out that new constitutions of choice are almost always parliamentary in character and not "presidential." I think a proper response to that is to point out that the American political system is not, in fact, presidential. It is a separation of powers system, which has quite different implications, it seems to me, for the way in which interests sort themselves out in the polity. Europeans call it a compound republic, because we've not only got a separation of powers, we've also got federalism, and we've got a strong judiciary to vindicate rights conferred on the populace by a Bill of

Rights. To me the most interesting edge of that whole thing is the extent to which the European community is tacitly, more than explicitly, but unmistakably, evolving toward imitation of us, because they've got the same kind of multiple system. They are about the same size. The other thing, of course, which is terribly important—I was at a wonderful conference once with mostly Brits, but some other people mixed in, and one guy, a person whose work you should know—Alan Ware, a great student of American parties and the history of American parties, two books into a great career—wrote a paper in which he said we have much to learn from small places, and he started going into how they do things in Malta and Iceland, so I took the opportunity to say, "You know, I've been thinking of writing a book about that, but I've only gotten as far as the title—*Pissant Democracy.*" You can put your arms all the way around Norway, but you can't in the United States, and that makes a tremendous difference in what burdens you can expect to put on various institutions. So as far as the exportability of American way of doing business constitutionally, my view is that the EU (European Union) is a primary place where they ought explicitly to be looking carefully at pluses and minuses, the way we do business. India, Russia, Brazil, Indonesia, and China, maybe. That's it. And of course, a fair number of those places, if you ask what is the size of the political elite—say, in China, for example—you can get them in this room. In other words, it would portend a considerable change.

One of the best books on this subject, you probably know it, is the memoir of Allan Gotlieb, who was a Canadian ambassador to the United States, published about ten years ago, maybe. He was an American trained lawyer, as it happens, a very learned fellow, and he said, "You know, before I became ambassador I never realized how important Congress was." This is a man who lives within the range of the Buffalo TV stations and all of the rest. We live in a condition of pluralistic ignorance, where mostly we don't know anything about one another.

Question: You have brought up the disadvantages of the blogosphere. Do you think the rise of the Internet in political communications is bad?

Polsby: A piece of technology is morally neutral. Its uses are subject to historical circumstance. I would say there are many occasions where the fact that issues can raised by, in effect, the welling up of sentiment, which is what it would amount to, might very well be a very good thing. On the other hand, it might not. That's the way it goes.

Chapter Six

Cultural Issues and the Future of the American Party System

William G. Mayer

This paper is about the following questions:

- ❖ How did affirmative action and racial preference policies become an established feature of American life, widely practiced by universities, corporations, and government agencies, even though polls repeatedly show that a substantial majority of Americans oppose such policies?
- ❖ How did the United States come to have some of the most permissive abortion laws anywhere in the world, even though the American public is highly ambivalent about abortion and, at most, moderately pro-choice?
- ❖ How is it that religion has been banished from large sectors of the public sphere, and operates under considerable suspicion in many other areas, even though the United States is, particularly in comparative terms, a remarkably religious country, in which most Americans say that religion is very important in their own lives?
- ❖ Why were the laws and rules of criminal procedure changed in ways that made it significantly more difficult to convict and incarcerate those accused of serious crimes, even though, at almost exactly the same time, crime rates were exploding and a substantial majority of Americans were complaining that the courts were treating criminals too leniently?

Race, abortion, religion, and crime are all examples of what are generally called social, cultural, or "values" issues. And as the title of this paper indicates, my ultimate aim is to talk about what role cultural issues play in the contemporary party system and what implications that has for the future of American politics. But in order to get to that, I first need to spend some time talking about the general characteristics of cultural politics. For as I hope to show, many of the generalizations we routinely make about American politics—as well as politics in other countries—were developed largely with reference to economic issues. When we turn to cultural issues, however, these generalizations no longer hold. Put simply, cultural politics is a very different game than economic politics, with different actors, different rules, and a distinct pattern of outcomes.

In particular, I want to argue, cultural politics is played on a very uneven field. The game of cultural politics is played under a set of rules that, in a post-industrial society like the United States, systematically advantages the cultural left. All of which helps explain the otherwise anomalous results mentioned a few minutes earlier: the spread of affirmative action, the liberalization of abortion laws, the enforced privatization of religion—even though there is, by and large, little evidence of a substantial public demand for such policies.

The Dynamics of Cultural Politics

Cultural issues are easy to define by example, much more difficult to define in general terms. Perhaps the best quick definition is the one offered by Ben Wattenberg: They are "what are left over after economics and foreign policy have been taken off the table."[1] In somewhat more positive terms, cultural issues are those matters of political dispute that are concerned less with the production and regulation of such tangible, bread-and-butter goods as jobs, housing, food, and medical care than with the moral values and standards that govern our lives. Besides race, religion, abortion, and crime, other examples of cultural issues include gay rights, immigration, drugs, patriotism, gun control, feminism, and pornography.

As I've already indicated, I believe that the basic dynamics of American cultural politics over the last fifty years have systematically advantaged those on the liberal side of the cultural issue spectrum. To be specific, cultural liberals have had four major factors working in their favor: participation, money, the media, and the judiciary.

Participation. One of the best-documented regularities in all of political science is the correlation between socioeconomic status and political participation. As a score of good studies have shown, those who rank higher on the status ladder— in particular, people with higher incomes and greater formal education— participate at higher levels than those with lower incomes and less education.[2] And, scholars who study these issues invariably note, this means that those most in favor of left-wing economic policies—welfare, redistribution, full employment, social security—have less of a voice in choosing our public officials and influencing public policy. As Sidney Verba and Norman Nie stated the problem more than three decades ago, "The political leader who thought he was learning about the attitudes of the public by observing the preferences of those activists around him, or the preferences of the citizens who come forward to contact him . . . would be receiving an inaccurate impression of the population as a whole. This is particularly the case in relation to economic issues relevant to welfare."[3]

What is almost never noted is that, when it comes to cultural issues, the ideological polarities are reversed. Simply put, cultural liberalism is the creed of the privileged classes. Support for legalized abortion, affirmative action, busing, feminism, and gay rights, opposition to school prayer, the death penalty, and a flag burning amendment are all strongly and positively correlated with both income and education. Hence, in general, the cultural left will out-participate the cultural right.

To put this proposition to the test, I have used data from what are generally regarded as the two premier academic social science surveys—the University of Michigan's American National Election Studies (ANES) and the University of Chicago's General Social Surveys (GSS). From both surveys, I have selected two types of questions.[4] The first was a series of measures of political participation, including voting, working in campaigns, contributing money, and contacting public officials. The second set of questions all dealt specifically with cultural policy issues: abortion, gay rights, capital punishment, gun control, pornography, drugs, immigration, and civil liberties. I then cross-tabulated the two types of variables, to see if the liberal position on each policy question was positively correlated with higher levels of participation.

The bottom line is that the cultural left out-participated the cultural right in 84 percent of the 239 cases I examined. To get a better sense of what these data look like, consider Table 6.1, which deals with an issue of some currency: immigration. As can be seen at the bottom of the table, in the 2004 ANES, as in virtually every other survey on this topic I've seen, American public opinion was stacked pretty decisively against immigration. Only 10 percent of the sample

Table 6.1. Political Participation in 2004 by Attitudes on Immigration (in percentages)

Number of immigrants from other countries should be

	Increased	Left Same	Decreased
Tried to influence others how to vote	53	45	50
Attended political meeting or rally	15	9	5
Displayed campaign button or bumper sticker	22	20	21
Did other work for party or candidate	6	4	2
Made political contribution	23	19	13
Voted	85	80	76
Worked with others on community problem	43	32	23
Contacted public official to express views	26	25	16
Attended community meeting	44	31	20
Took part in protest march or demonstration	9	4	2
Approx. N	(106)	(450)	(491)

Source: ANES 2004

Note: Results of the immigration question for the full sample were: increased, 10 percent; left same, 42 percent; decreased, 46 percent; don't know, 1 percent.

wanted to increase the number of immigrants from other countries, 46 percent favored a reduction. So why is Washington now considering a variety of proposals to *expand* immigration?

One answer may be that elected officials respond not to the American public as a whole, but to that much smaller part of it that actively participates. Of the nine forms of participation shown in this table, immigration supporters outparticipated opponents on every one of them. In some cases, such as voting and displaying a campaign button, the difference is not terribly large; but on the more demanding and probably more influential forms of activity, the gap becomes quite substantial. Those who wanted to increase the level of immigration were about twice as likely to make a political contribution or attend a community meeting as those who sought to reduce the flow of immigrants, about three times as likely to attend a political meeting or do other work for a party or candidate, and more than four times as likely to take part in a protest march.

One of the few consistent exceptions to the general pattern noted here—it is worth calling attention to because it is an exception to several of the generalizations discussed in this paper—is gun control. In both the ANES and GSS data, opponents of gun control participate at higher levels than proponents.[5]

Money. Of all the participatory advantages that accrue to cultural liberalism, one particularly deserves to be singled out: money. If cultural liberals are, on average, both wealthier and more politically involved than cultural conservatives, it should come as no great surprise to find that the groups and causes affiliated with the cultural left are, in general, better funded than their conservative counterparts. Again, I want to underline the difference between cultural issues and economic issues. The image that we're all familiar with, in which parties on the political right raise more money than those on the left, is grounded in the two groups' relative positions on economic questions. Though there are more exceptions than is often recognized, in general businesses tend to support what are usually thought of as conservative economic policies, labor unions are more often allied with liberal and left-wing parties, and since business owners and management have more money at their disposal than ordinary laborers, Republican candidates, at least after taking incumbency into account, can usually outraise their Democratic counterparts.

But cultural politics marches to a different drummer. As anyone located near Hollywood should know all too well, there is a lot of money on the cultural left, far more than among the sorts of people and groups that make up the bulk of cultural traditionalists. Unfortunately for my purposes, most of the money that is donated and spent in American politics does not come clearly labeled such that we can tell whether it was motivated by economic or cultural concerns or some combination of the two. We know, for example, that then-governor George W. Bush raised an enormous amount of money for the 2000 presidential nomination race, considerably more than a sitting vice president with the full force of the White House behind him—but there is no obvious way of saying how much of that money came from economic conservatives, how much from cultural conservatives, and how much from people for whom ideology and issues frankly didn't matter that much.

Still, there are a number of ways of getting some kind of empirical purchase on this question. One way is to examine the donation records of political action committees (PACs), many of which do make clear, in their names or statements of purpose, that they are concerned primarily or exclusively with cultural issues. The Center for Responsive Politics, for example, compiles data every two years showing the total amounts of money given to federal candidates by pro-choice and pro-life PACs. In each of the last four election cycles, which are the only ones currently listed on the Center's website, the pro-choice committees substantially out-contributed the pro-life PACs, by an average margin of about 2.3 to 1. In 2004, for example, pro-choice PACs contributed $1,175,000, 87 percent of it to Democrats; pro-life committees donated just $563,000, 98 percent to Republicans.[6]

Or to take another comparison, gay rights and left-wing feminist PACs contributed about $1,655,000 during the 2004 election cycle. My best attempt to come up with a conservative equivalent to these groups—PACs with a special commitment to traditional values and Republican women candidates—indicates that during the same period, these groups gave only about $439,000. Again, gun control forms an interesting exception to this pattern: Anti-gun control groups give substantially more money than proponents. Still, when everything is taken into account, my estimate—which, I should caution, I'm still in the process of refining—is that in the average recent election cycle, left-wing cultural PACs have contributed about 30 percent more money than right-wing cultural PACs.

Media. The third factor working in favor of the cultural left is the bias of the American news media. As you're no doubt aware, there is, by now, a quite substantial literature dealing with the subject of media bias. One large part of it, generally though not invariably written by conservatives, claims that the media have a liberal bias. Another large part, mostly written by liberals, accuses the media of having a conservative bias. After an extensive review of this literature, it is my conclusion that those who argue that the media have a liberal bias have considerably the better of the argument. Most of the books and articles that allege a right-wing media bias are long on theory and short on evidence, and such evidence as they do produce often turns out to be unreliable.[7] In a speech of this length, however, there is no way I can do justice to the depth and complexity of this question, so instead let me make a couple of points that relate specifically to the issue of how the media deal with cultural issues.

For those who accuse the media of a liberal tilt, Exhibit A is the surveys that have been taken of reporters, editors, and producers, which almost invariably show such people to be substantially more liberal than the American adult population as a whole. What has not received sufficient attention, however, is that the liberalness of those who work for the media varies quite a bit according to the particular type of issue that is being examined.

On economic issues, the media are, in fact, not that much more liberal than the general population. Perhaps the single best study of the media's political attitudes was conducted a number of years ago by Bill Schneider and I.A. Lewis, who posed an identical set of questions to two national samples: one of the general public, the other a sample of reporters and editors.[8] When asked whether they sided more with business or labor, 27 percent of the reporters and editors said business, as compared to 33 percent of the general public. Eighty-three percent of the public said that government should aid those unable to support themselves; 95 percent of journalists took this position. One can find other questions that make the media look comparatively more liberal, but if all we had to go on were questions about economic issues, we would probably conclude that those who work for the media are slightly but not dramatically more liberal than their audience.

But this small gap becomes a chasm when we examine data on cultural issues. On cultural issues, it truly can be said that the media and their audience often seem to be members of separate societies. Using again the data from the Schneider-Lewis study, 49 percent of the American public said they favored allowing women to have legal abortions—but 82 percent of journalists took this position. Seventy-four percent of the public favored prayer in the public schools—as against just 25 percent of the media. On the issue of the death penalty, the general public endorsed it by a margin of better than 4-to-1: 75 percent in favor, 17 percent opposed. The media, by contrast, were split right down the middle: 47 percent in favor, 47 percent against. Differences of 25 or 30 percentage points also show up in questions about affirmative action, gun control, and hiring homosexuals.

Faced with these types of data, those who claim the media have a right-wing bias generally reply by saying that the personal attitudes of journalists are less important than the nature of the organizations they work for, and that the most significant fact about contemporary news is that it is gathered and reported by large, for-profit corporations, who consequently have a vested interest in seeing that the news projects a favorable view of capitalism and corporations. There are, in my view, numerous problems with this argument, but the point I wish to make for the moment is that, even if we accept this claim, it suggests, at most, why the media might have a conservative take on economic issues. Even in theory, it does not explain—at least, not in any obvious way—why the media would oppose abortion, or favor prayer in the public schools, or line up in opposition to gun control.

In fact, as numerous good studies have demonstrated, the media have generally—not always, but in most cases—been reliable allies of cultural liberals, framing events in ways that are sympathetic to liberal causes, using language favored by liberal groups while rejecting the preferred terminology of conservatives, showing considerably more inclination to pursue investigative stories that portray conservative causes and groups in an unfavorable light than similar stories about liberals.[9]

The Judiciary. One final factor that has clearly advantaged cultural liberals over the last fifty years has been the pattern of judicial decisions. Make a list of the major victories won by the cultural left since the early 1950s, and you have to be impressed by how many of them were achieved, not because new legislation was enacted by democratically accountable legislatures and chief executives, but because of court decisions, particularly decisions by the U.S. Supreme Court, in which they declared long-standing laws and practices that were supportive of traditional moral values to be unconstitutional. Obvious examples include abortion, school prayer, criminal procedure, pornography, busing, vagrancy and public order, flag burning, gay marriage, and, for a brief period of time, the death penalty.

Many legal scholars and liberal activists would reply that while liberals have indeed used the courts to pursue their policy goals, conservatives are guilty of much the same behavior. Liberal presidents appoint liberal judges, conservative presidents appoint conservatives (or at least they try to). Both groups bring their ideological convictions into play when they interpret the Constitution. So what's all the fuss about?

But this sort of "judicial equivalency" ignores one fundamental difference between the way that liberal and conservative judges have gone about their task over the last half century, at least on cultural issues. The central thrust of liberal judicial philosophy has been to expand the number and scope of what liberals view as basic rights, and thus to remove these issues from resolution by the ordinary processes of democratic decision-making. Conservatives, by contrast, have taken a much narrower view of such rights, and thus reserve a far larger and more powerful role for the democratic branches of government. In this sense, liberal and conservative approaches to cultural questions are decidedly not mirror images of each other: They have dramatically different direct effects. Liberal decisions guarantee the implementation of liberal cultural policies. Conservative decisions, however, merely give elected officials the option of legislating conservative policies. Liberal decisions thus limit the sphere of democratic decision-making, conservative decisions work to expand it.

Take abortion as an example. Setting compromises aside, there are three "pure" positions that the courts might adopt for dealing with this issue:

1. They could rule that the mother's right to have an abortion if she wants one is constitutionally protected, and that legislatures have no power to interfere with that right.
2. They could rule that the fetus's right to life is constitutionally protected, and that legislatures have no power to interfere with that right.
3. They could rule that the constitution says nothing one way or the other about abortion, and that the matter should therefore be left to the decision of state and/or national legislatures, to settle as they think best.

Number 1 is, of course, the consensus liberal position, as adopted in *Roe v. Wade*. But number 2 is definitely not the mainstream conservative position.

There are a few conservative legal scholars who have made such an argument, but they are clearly minority voices.[10] The vast majority of conservatives— including, so far as one can tell, every one of the conservative justices now serving on the U.S. Supreme Court—have embraced position number three. In that sense, though you would never know it from the way the issue is generally reported in the media, the overturning of *Roe v. Wade* will not mean that abortion will be illegal. It will merely mean that the states have the option of outlawing abortion—an option that many states plainly will not take, at least in near future.

The same logic applies to the liberal and conservative stances on gay marriage, capital punishment, the rights of the accused, and the role of religion in public life. Indeed, the only exception to this pattern in the realm of cultural politics that I have been able to think of is affirmative action. In every other case, judicial conservatives would allow legislatures and executives to settle these matters as they choose; liberal justices would forbid elected officials from adopting any policy except the one the judges themselves prefer.

Again, in a lengthier speech, I would amplify and develop this argument in considerably more detail. For now, let me just add one other observation: There is, I believe, nothing inherent in the liberal or conservative philosophies of government that indissolubly links them with either an active or limited role for the judiciary. Indeed, as anyone familiar with the history of the Supreme Court knows, from the late 1800s through the mid-1930s, the positions of the two ideologies were largely reversed. During the Progressive Era and the early years of the New Deal, it was conservatives who wanted the Court to protect what they regarded as basic economic rights and thus limit what legislatures could do by way of intervening in economic affairs. Liberals were content to settle such issues through the democratic process and thus sought a considerably more limited role for the judiciary.

Indeed, the farther left one went, the more critical early twentieth century Americans were of judicial meddling. The 1912 Progressive Party convention that nominated Theodore Roosevelt also adopted a platform that demanded "such restriction of the power of the courts as shall leave to the people the ultimate authority to determine fundamental questions of social welfare and public policy." This was to be accomplished by, among other things, allowing state court decisions to be overridden by popular referendum and by making the U.S. Constitution easier to amend. In a similar vein, Robert LaFollette's platform of 1924 declared, "The usurpation in recent years by the federal courts of the power to nullify laws duly enacted by the legislative branch of the government is a plain violation of the Constitution." His preferred remedies were allowing Congress to override judicial decisions by statute and having federal judges popularly elected for ten-year terms.[11] The remarkable change in the left's attitude toward judicial power says volumes about the lack of popular support for many of its cultural policies.

Implications for the Party System

The analysis presented thus far has several significant implications for the present and future course of the American party system. Most importantly, it underlines the fragile yet functional nature of the Republican coalition. Economic and cultural conservatives may not be natural allies, and both may spend time complaining that they sacrifice too much and get too little in return, but on balance, both groups reap substantial benefits from the partnership.

The most important thing that economic conservatives contribute to the coalition is money: Without the support of business, candidates who support conservative cultural policies would be substantially underfunded in comparison with their liberal opponents. And what do cultural conservatives add to the party? The simple answer is: votes. When Republicans were simply the party of economic conservatism, as they were from the early 1930s to the late 1960s, they were also distinctly the minority party. It was only when they added the allegiance of cultural conservatives that Republicans were able to win presidential and then congressional elections on a regular basis. Though I don't have time to demonstrate it here, I think the evidence shows that the Republicans have been a net winner on most cultural issues. Moving substantially to the left on cultural issues might gain the party a few additional votes in New Jersey and California, but it would also create huge problems for the party in large parts of the South, the Midwest, and the non-Pacific West.

Specific policies aside, cultural issues help—or at least could help— Republicans in one other important way. Every four years since 1952, the American National Election Studies have included a set of questions asking people what they like and dislike about the two major parties. As these data make clear, the most significant advantage the Democrats have had for the last 50 years—indeed, probably ever since the dawn of the New Deal—is that they are seen as the party of the common person, the average worker, the "little guy," while Republicans are seen as overly beholden to the rich, the well born, and the big corporations. Properly used, there is some indication that cultural issues have at least some capacity to counteract this set of images: to make the Democrats seem like a more elitist party, while allowing Republicans to assume a somewhat more populist mantle.

Ironically, in light of these potential advantages, one recurrent challenge for the Republican Party has been its reluctance to raise and campaign on cultural issues. Over the last several decades, virtually every time Republicans have tried to make a cultural issue a major focus of a campaign, they have faced a flood of unfavorable media coverage, in editorials and op-ed columns but also in so-called straight news pieces, claiming that the issue is unfair, unimportant, divisive, or mean-spirited.

The archetypal example of this quandary was the Willie Horton-furlough issue in 1988. By all accounts, this issue was quite successful in convincing lots of Americans that Michael Dukakis was, in fact, a liberal, and that his position on crime and other cultural issues was substantially to the left of the average voter.

Yet, even as the Bush campaign was opening up a significant lead in the polls, they faced a flood of highly critical commentary, arguing that the issue was racist, misleading, and irrelevant. Bush won the election, of course, but in the long run, the Republicans lost the war. I am now in the process of doing a content analysis of media references to Willie Horton in the years since 1988, and I have, to this point, two notable findings: one, that the issue is raised more often by Democrats than by Republicans; and second, that Horton's name is often used as a synonym for an unfair attack. In 1992, for example, Bill Clinton responded to some of the GOP attacks against his wife by accusing the Republicans of "trying to make it kind of a Willie Horton-like thing against all independent, working women." More generally, noted *The New York Times,* "Willie Horton is emerging as the Democrats' most potent rhetorical weapon, with supporters of Gov. Bill Clinton gleefully dropping his name as often as they recall President Bush's 'no new taxes' pledge."[12]

In a similar way, when George W. Bush finally announced in the summer of 2004 that he would support a constitutional amendment defining marriage as a union between a man and a woman, the dominant theme in the editorials and commentary pieces I have examined was not just that he was wrong on the issue, but that the whole subject was somehow an illegitimate one to bring up in the context of a presidential campaign, motivated not by sincere policy convictions but only by the crassest political calculations. As the *Los Angeles Times* put it, "There's no crisis here, only a president bent on dividing a nation that is otherwise more concerned about war and jobs." The *Chicago Sun-Times* declared, "The only reason to involve the federal government [in marriage-related issues] is due to unfortunate—and possibly self-defeating—political motives. Basically, it's a waste of time." "The efforts [to amend the Constitution]," added the *Kansas City Star,* "are politically motivated and divisive. President Bush's" recent announcement "appears to be an unfortunate attempt to create a wedge issue to bolster his re-election campaign."[13]

Of course, cultural issues are divisive, as are economic and foreign policy issues, but they are divisive not because they are being artificially created and manipulated by politicians, but because they represent real and significant disagreements about how we live our lives and the moral values and standards we revere and cherish. And where such disagreements exist, we are better off settling them through the give and take of public debate rather than by sweeping them under the table for the decision of unaccountable elites. Or, such at any rate, has always been the faith of democracy.

Questions and Answers

Question: You say that the reason liberal positions prevail on most social issues is because the factors you describe advantage the cultural left. But another explanation might be that on almost all those issues, the position that wins is usually one where the benefits are concentrated on a rather narrow group, and the costs are widely dispersed. The exception is gun control, but as you say, that's one issue where conservatives tend to out-give and out-participate liberals.

William Mayer: That's an interesting question, concerning an aspect of these issues that I never thought about. One response I would make is to say the support for liberal social positions is not by any means limited to those who might be described as their beneficiaries. Support for gay marriage, for example, is not limited to gays and lesbians who think they might like to get married. The support for dropping the words "under God" from the Pledge of Allegiance is not concentrated solely among atheists with children of school age. Most cultural issues, almost by definition, deal with intangibles. Who supports abortion, for example? It's not just women who might want to have abortions or men who might want their spouses or girlfriends to get one. Many women I know who would never contemplate getting an abortion themselves—or who are well past child-bearing age—nevertheless would view it as philosophically offensive if government were to tell women what they could or could not do with their bodies—or at least, that's the way they view the issue.

Question: Isn't the real reason that anti-abortion laws don't get enacted is that abortion is a losing position, and people who espouse the pro-life side just don't get elected?

Mayer: Not in this state [California], but there are lots of states that routinely elect pro-life Republicans to various kinds of positions, including governors and U.S. senators.

Question: But their policy impact is nil.

Mayer: Well, but of course, one reason why their policy impact, in fact, is nil is because of the point I made, namely, that judicial decisions have had the tendency to substantially advantage the left. I agree that in a typical state, the range of allowable things you can do about abortion at the moment is rather narrow, at least unless you want to pass something like the South Dakota legislature did recently, that it passed solely for the purpose of creating a challenge to *Roe vs. Wade.* But where the issue does still matter, I would argue, is in the appointment of federal judges.

Question: Then why does it matter who contributes to whom?

Mayer: Well, we do elect presidents. We nominate them, and as we have found out by comparing the reception that Alito got, versus the reception that Bork got, it really does matter whether you have the majority of your own party in the U.S. Senate. I think abortion is an important issue even for the House. Given that the range of things have been substantially narrowed, there are still things that the court probably would allow—for example, parental consent laws. I think it's a much more substantial issue in terms of the Senate and the presidency.

Question: Hasn't the anti-abortion right pushed a lot of Republican candidates to take a stronger pro-life position that they were inclined to?

Mayer: What I would argue is everything you've just said about the Republican Party is true of the Democratic Party in the opposite direction. Richard Gephardt was once a pro-life Democrat. He switched his position when he decided he was going to run for president. I'm not sure that you and I are necessarily disagreeing here, because I think the basic point is it underlies the significance of cultural issues to people.

Question: Don't Republicans have to move away from the pro-life position to be competitive in states like California and New York?

Mayer: I don't disagree that being pro-life is not a winning position in California. There are a number of other states I could point to where it's not either, but if you look at all at the question of where the public is on abortion, there are very few issues where survey question wording matters as much. At least my fairest reading of it is that the number of clearly pro-choice and pro-life people is less than a majority, and the majority is somewhere in the middle, and is quite ambivalent, and may not even know quite what they want.

Question: What does this issue say about the role of the judiciary in American politics?

Mayer: If I were giving a longer talk about the role of the judiciary I would argue for a considerably more limited role. That, incidentally, was not my purpose here. I was really making a much more descriptive point that court decisions have been a major source of victories for the cultural left in this country.

Notes

1. See the discussion in Ben J. Wattenberg, *Values Matter Most* (New York: Free Press, 1995), 15–18. The definition quoted in the text appears on p. 15.
2. Perhaps the classic analysis of the relationship appears in Sidney Verba and Norman H. Nie, *Participation in America: Political Democracy and Social Equality* (New York: Harper & Row, 1972). For a good recent review of the research, see Arend Lijphart, "Unequal Participation: Democracy's Unresolved Dilemma," *American Political Science Review* 91 (March 1997): 1–14.
3. Verba and Nie, *Participation in America*, 284. See also Alexander Keyssar, *The Right to Vote: The Contested History of Democracy in the United States* (New York: Basic Books, 2000), 320.
4. For the General Social Survey, all data come the 1987 survey, the only GSS that included an extensive set of questions dealing with political participation. For the Ameri-

can National Election Studies, all data come from the 2004 survey, though I now extending the analysis back through earlier years.

5. For a similar finding with regard to gun control, see Howard Schuman and Stanley Presser, *Questions and Answers in Attitude Surveys: Experiments on Question Form, Wording, and Context* (New York: Academic Press, 1981), chap. 9.

6. All data are taken from www.opensecrets.org/pacs (viewed March 29, 2006).

7. For an intensive review of two such books—Herbert Gans, *Deciding What's News* and Ben Bagdikian, *The Media Monopoly*—see William G. Mayer, "What Conservative Media? The Unproven Case for Conservative Media Bias," *Critical Review* (forthcoming).

8. All of the data in the next two paragraphs are taken from Table 1 in William Schneider and I. A. Lewis, "Views on the News," *Public Opinion*, August/September 1985, 7.

9. The literature on this topic is voluminous, but see, in particular, David Shaw, "Abortion Bias Seeps into News," *Los Angeles Times*, July 1-4, 1990; Louis Bolce and Gerald De Maio, "The Politics of Partisan Neutrality," *First Things* 143 (May 2004): 9-12; and S. Robert Lichter, Stanley Rothman, and Linda S. Lichter, *The Media Elite* (New York: Hastings House, 1986), chap. 7.

10. See, for example, Nathan Schlueter, "Constitutional Persons: An Exchange," *First Things* 129 (January 2003): 28-36. See also, however, the rejoinder by Robert H. Bork.

11. For the texts of the two platforms, see Donald Bruce Johnson, ed., *National Party Platforms*, vol. 2, *1840–1956* (Urbana: University of Illinois Press, 1978), 176 and 252, 254.

12. Both quotes are taken from Richard L. Berke, "In 1992, Willie Horton is Democrats' Weapon," *New York Times*, August 25, 1992, A18.

13. *Los Angeles Times*, February 26, 2004; *Chicago Sun-Times*, February 26, 2004; and *Kansas City Star*, February 28, 2004. For other examples, see *Editorials on File*, March 16-31, 2004.

Bibliography

Berke, Richard L. "In 1992, Willie Horton is Democrats' Weapon." *New York Times*, August 25, 1992, A18.

Bolce, Louis and Gerald De Maio. "The Politics of Partisan Neutrality." *First Things* 143 (May 2004): 9–12.

Johnson, Donald Bruce, ed. *National Party Platforms*, vol. 2, *1840-1956*. Urbana: University of Illinois Press, 1978.

Keyssar, Alexander. *The Right to Vote: The Contested History of Democracy in the United States*. New York: Basic Books, 2000.

Lichter, S. Robert, Stanley Rothman, and Linda S. Lichter. *The Media Elite*. New York: Hastings House, 1986.

Lijphart, Arend. "Unequal Participation: Democracy's Unresolved Dilemma." *American Political Science Review* 91 (March 1997): 1–14.

Mayer, William G. "What Conservative Media? The Unproven Case for Conservative Media Bias." *Critical Review* (forthcoming).

"Political Action Committees," www.opensecrets.org/pacs (viewed March 29, 2006).

Schlueter, Nathan. "Constitutional Persons: An Exchange." *First Things* 129 (January 2003): 28-36.

Schneider, William and I.A. Lewis. "Views on the News." *Public Opinion,* August/September 1985.

Schuman, Howard and Stanley Presser. *Questions and Answers in Attitude Surveys: Experiments on Question Form, Wording, and Context.* New York: Academic Press, 1981.

Shaw, David. "Abortion Bias Seeps into News." *Los Angeles Times,* July 1–4, 1990.

Verba, Sidney and Norman H. Nie. *Participation in America: Political Democracy and Social Equality.* New York: Harper & Row, 1972.

Wattenberg, Ben J. *Values Matter Most.* New York: Free Press, 1995.

Index

9-11, 4, 6, 24, 30, 40, 45, 51–52, 68–75, 79
527 committees, 15, 31, 95

abortion issue, 9, 19, 22, 29, 38–39, 58, 64, 107–9, 111, 113–18
Abramoff, Jack. *see* lobbying scandal
Abu Ghraib, 77
affirmative action issue, 54, 107–9, 112, 114
Afghanistan war, 33, 72, 75
Alexander, Lamar, 59
Alito, Samuel, 53
Allen, George, 73, 78
American exceptionalism, 29–31, 63, 66, 76–79

bankruptcy issue, 15
Berman, Howard, 32
Bipartisan Campaign Reform Act (BCRA), 83–98
black voters, 6, 39, 54, 59, 67
Blair, Tony, 13, 31
blogosphere, 7, 12, 20, 27, 36, 49, 51, 77, 100, 103, 105
Boxer, Barbara, 11
Bradley, Bill, 92
Brownback, Sam, 73
budget deficit issue, 5, 39–40, 55–56, 59, 68, 78–79
Bush, George H. W., 9, 57, 73, 89, 116
Bush, George W., 2–3, 5, 7, 10–11, 14, 16–17, 27–28, 32, 36, 40, 50–59, 61–69, 72–73, 77–79, 90, 92, 110, 116
campaign finance reform, 28–29, 93–97, 101. *See also* Bipartisan Campaign Reform Act
Casey, Bob, 19
Chaffee, Lincoln, 19
civil society, 53, 59
Clinton, Bill, 2, 5–9, 11, 13–16, 23, 25, 31, 50, 54–56, 62, 70–73, 76, 78, 89, 116
Clinton, Hillary, 15, 18, 27, 61, 70, 73
compassionate conservatism, 21, 51, 53–58, 64
competence issue, 2, 4–5, 11, 18, 21, 40

conservatism, 2–3, 5, 7, 11, 16, 40, 49–50, 53–61, 67, 73, 111–17
Constitution, 17, 53–55, 58, 100, 116
Contract with America, 17, 22–23
corruption issue, 24–25, 50, 55. *See also* lobbying scandal
crime issue, 8, 64, 107–11, 113–17
cultural issues, 7–10, 21, 57–58, 65, 67–68, 107–120

Daley, Richard, 77
Daschle, Tom, 16
Dean, Howard, 15, 27, 46–47, 50, 72, 94; and fifty-state strategy, 19, 25–26, 47
death penalty issue. *See* crime issue
Democratic Leadership Council (DLC), 11–12, 20
Democratic Party, 1–34, 35–47, 50–52, 57–58, 60–70, 73–74, 76–80, 83–91, 94–96, 101–4, 111, 116
demographics, 20, 50, 60, 65–67, 71
Dewey, Thomas, 71
Dubai ports deal, 7, 40, 45
Dukakis, Michael, 4, 9, 89, 115–16
Durbin, Richard, 77

economic performance, 69, 78–79
education issue, 53, 56
Edwards, John, 111, 73
Eisenhower, Dwight, 54, 69, 71
election of *1912*, 114; *1924*, 114; *1946*, 40, 69–71; *1948*, 63, 71; *1952*, 57, 63, 71–72, 74; *1960*, 63; *1964*, 69, 73; *1968*, 69, 74; *1980*, 69; *1984*, 56–57; *1986*, 69; *1988*, 4, 9, 11, 13, 57, 89, 115–16; *1992*, 5, 7, 11, 57, 69, 71, 78, 116; *1994*, 22–25, 49–50, 54, 56, 61, 67, 69, 71, 80, 88; *1996*, 57, 70, 78, 88–89; *2000*, 4, 6, 7, 9–10, 56, 70–71, 78, 87, 92, 110; *2002*, 6, 49, 51, 54, 84, 87; *2004*, 1, 6, 7, 9, 12–14, 20, 26, 28, 49, 51–54, 56–57, 63–67, 69–72, 83–87, 90–92, 94–95, 116; *2006*, 1, 19, 23–24, 41, 45–46, 50, 68–71, 79–81, 95–96; *2008*, 1, 6, 12, 30, 46, 65, 70–74, 78
Emmanuel, Rahm, 25

Enron scandal, 22
environment issue, 9, 28, 39

faith-based services, 10
Federal Election Campaign Act, 89
Federal Emergency Management
    Agency, 5, 18
Feingold, Russ, 16, 27, 68, 73, 95
flag burning issue, 108, 113
foreign policy issue, 2, 5–7, 10, 13, 15–
    16, 18, 21, 31–32, 40–42, 45, 51–
    52, 59–60, 63–64, 66, 68, 71–72,
    76–78
Frist, Bill, 61, 73
fundraising, 9–10, 83–98, 110–11;
    internet fundraising, 9–10, 27, 37,
    86, 92–93, 98; state parties, 83, 87

gay rights issue, 9, 28–29, 58, 108–9,
    111, 112–14, 116–17
Gephardt, Richard, 13, 118
gerrymandering, 25, 79–80
Gingrich, Newt, 17, 23–24, 40–41, 51,
    69, 71, 73
Giuliani, Rudy, 70–73, 78
globalization. See trade issue
Goldwater, Barry, 49–51, 55, 57, 69, 73
Gore, Al, 2, 4, 6–7, 9–10, 27, 63, 72–
    73, 92
government shutdowns, 4, 23
Guantanamo Bay, 77
gun control issue, 108–9, 111–12

Hart, Gary, 8
Hastert, Dennis, 61
health care issue, 3–4, 11, 13, 17, 38,
    50, 64, 71
Hispanic voters, 28, 39, 54, 56, 59–60,
    67, 74–76
Hollywood, 9–10, 29, 110
Homeland Security, Department of, 5–
    6, 18
Huckabee, Mike, 73
human rights issue, 31–32
Humphrey, Hubert, 76, 104
Hurricane Katrina, 4–5, 23, 40

immigration issue, 12–13, 59–60, 67,
    74–76, 109–10
interest groups, 19, 99–100

Internet. See blogosphere; fundraising;
    new media; party organization
Iran issue, 72, 78
Iraq war issue, 4–7, 15–16, 18, 27, 30–
    31, 41, 45, 51, 68, 72–73, 77–78

Jeffords, James, 49, 69
Johnson, Lyndon, 2, 5
judiciary, 38, 50, 53, 68, 70, 90, 108,
    113–14, 117–18

Kaine, Tim, 5,8
Kennedy, Edward, 8, 11, 15
Kennedy, John, 63
Kennedy, Robert, 36
Kerry, John, 4, 6, 14–16, 27–28, 31, 53,
    63–67, 73
Kosovo war, 13

La Follette, Robert, 114
labor unions, 4, 50, 66
liberalism, 7, 12, 15, 31–32, 46, 49–50,
    52, 56, 60, 65, 76, 108–14, 116–17
Lieberman, Joseph, 2, 10, 72
Lincoln, Abraham, 36–37
lobbying scandal, 25, 55, 67

married voters, 7, 67
McCain, John, 70, 73, 78, 95
McConnell v. Federal Election
    Commission, 90
McGovern–Fraser Commission
    reforms, 26–27, 100–102
McGovern, George, 50
media, 100, 108, 111–12, 115–16. See
    also new media
Medicaid, 1
Medicare, 1, 4, 6, 17, 53, 55–56, 64
Moore, Michael, 68, 76–77
Mondale, Walter, 50
moral values issues. See cultural issues
MoveOn.org, 12, 39, 50, 68
Murtha, John, 68

National Religious Partnership for the
    Environment, 9
Netroots. See Internet
New Deal coalition, 69
new media, 49, 51, 53, 62, 66–69
Nixon, Richard, 63, 73
Nunn, Sam, 11

Obama, Barack, 13
Occupational Safety and Health
    Administration, 23
Ownership Society, 53, 59

party organization, 37–38, 49, 51, 99–
    105; internet organizing, 36; state
    party organization, 25–26, 100–
    101
PATRIOT Act, 16
Pelosi, Nancy, 32, 68, 70
pensions issue, 3–4, 14–15, 17, 64
Perot, H. Ross, 38, 57, 71
political reform, 42
poverty issue, 29, 39–40
prescription drugs. See Medicare

Rangel, Charles, 70
Reagan, Ronald, 49–50, 53, 55–60, 61,
    67–69, 73
religious issues, 2, 9–10, 18–19, 108,
    112–14, 117. See also cultural
    issues
religious voters, 9–11, 18–19, 28–29,
    39, 42; black religious voters, 28–
    29; Catholic voters, 28, 52, 65–
    66, 102; Evangelical voters, 9, 28,
    39, 102
Republican Party, 2, 7, 8–9, 14, 16–18,
    20–29, 37–38, 40, 46, 49–81, 83–
    91, 95–96, 101–02, 104, 111, 115–
    18
retirement programs, 60. See also
    Medicare; Social Security
Robb, Charles, 11

Roberts, John, 53
Roemer, Timothy, 10, 66, 69
Romney, Mitt, 73, 78
Roosevelt, Eleanor, 76
Roosevelt, Franklin, 2, 63, 76
Roosevelt, Theodore, 114
Rove, Karl, 40–41, 51
Rumsfeld, Donald, 41–42, 78

Santorum, Rick, 19
secular voters, 9, 28
Sharpton, Al, 73
social safety net, 2, 10, 12–13, 22
Social Security issue, 2–5, 11–12
Soros, George, 29
Supreme Court. See judiciary

Taft, Robert, 71
tax issue, 2, 4, 18, 20–21, 53, 56–58,
    68, 79
terrorism issue, 7–8, 31, 41–42, 52, 59,
    66
third parties, 36, 103–4
Thurmond, Strom, 71
trade issue, 4, 12–14, 43–45
Truman, Harry, 63, 65, 68, 71, 76

Ventura, Jesse, 103
voter participation, 62–63, 71, 108–110

Wallace, Henry, 71, 76
Warner, Mark, 11–12
welfare issue, 7, 54–55, 64, 108
women voters, 7–9, 20, 54, 56–57
working class voters, 13, 20

About the Participants

Michael Barone is currently senior writer for *U.S. News and World Report*, is the principal coauthor of the biennial *Almanac of American Politics*, and is widely considered one of the most knowledgeable analysts of American politics. He is also a frequent commentator on political news programs.

Peter Beinart is editor of *The New Republic,* one of the nation's oldest liberal journals of political opinion. He is also author of *The Good Fight: Why Liberals—And Only Liberals—Can Win the War on Terror and Make America Great Again*, and is a columnist for *Time* and the *Washington Post*.

Andrew E. Busch is professor of government and Salvatori Senior Research Fellow at Claremont McKenna College. He is also author or coauthor of numerous books on American politics, including *Red Over Blue: The 2004 Elections and American Politics*.

Patrick Caddell is a long-time Democratic campaign consultant who was instrumental in the presidential campaigns of George McGovern in 1972, Jimmy Carter in 1976 and 1980, and Gary Hart in 1984. He also served as a consultant to the television show *The West Wing*.

Hugh Hewitt has a nationally-syndicated radio show and is author of several books on American politics and new media, including *Painting the Map Red: The Fight to Create a Permanent Republican Majority*. He also teaches at Chapman University School of Law and served in numerous posts in the Reagan Administration.

Elaine Kamarck teaches at the John F. Kennedy School of Government at Harvard University. She worked in the Clinton White House from 1993–1997 and has been a key thinker in the "New Democrat" movement originally taking the form of the Democratic Leadership Council.

Charles Kesler is professor of government and director of the Salvatori Center for the Study of Individual Freedom in the Modern World at Claremont McKenna College. He also edited *Keeping the Tablets*: *Readings in American Conservatism* and is Editor of the *Claremont Review of Books*.

William Kristol is editor and publisher of *The Weekly Standard*, a prominent conservative journal of opinion and is a frequent commentator on Fox News and other venues. He previously served in the Reagan Administration and as Chief of Staff to Vice President Dan Quayle in the George H.W. Bush Administration.

Michael Malbin is executive director at the Campaign Finance Institute in Washington, D.C. He is also professor of political science at the State University of New York, Albany. He is author or coauthor of numerous books and chapters on Congress and campaign finance, including *The Election after Reform: Money, Politics and the Bipartisan Campaign Reform Act* and *Vital Statistics on Congress.*

William G. Mayer is associate professor of political science at Northeastern University in Boston, Massachusetts. He is editor and author of a number of works in American politics and public opinion, including *The Making of the Presidential Candidates 2004*, *The Changing American Mind*, and *The Front-Loading Problem in Presidential Nominations.*

Nelson W. Polsby was professor of political science at the University of California–Berkeley. He authored or coauthored a plethora of influential books on parties, elections, and American institutions, including *How Congress Evolves*, *Presidential Elections*, *Consequences of Party Reform*, and *New Federalist Papers*. He also edited several top political science journals, including the *American Political Science Review* and the *Annual Review of Political Science.*

Timothy Roemer served as a Democratic member of the U.S. House of Representatives from Indiana from 1991–2003. He also served on the bipartisan 9-11 commission. He is currently President of the Center for National Policy in Washington, D.C. and distinguished scholar at the Mercatus Center at George Mason University. He was a candidate for Chairman of the Democratic National Committee in 2005.

Ruy Teixeira is a joint fellow at the Center for American Progress and the Century Foundation in Washington, D.C. He is author of *The Disappearing American Voter*, America's *Forgotten Majority: Why the White Working Class Still Matters*, and (with John Judis) The *Emerging Democratic Majority.*